PLANTS
FOR THE
HOUSE AND PATIO

PLANTS
FOR THE
HOUSE AND PATIO

CREATING AN ATMOSPHERE

Explanation of plant glossary symbols

 Shady location

 Semi-shady location

 Sunny location

 Water sparingly

 Water normally

 Water liberally

 Fertilise sparingly

 Fertilise normally

 Fertilise liberally

© Naumann & Göbel Verlagsgesellschaft mbH, a subsidiary of
VEMAG Verlags- und Medien Aktiengesellschaft, Cologne
www.apollo-intermedia.de

Complete production: Naumann & Göbel Verlagsgesellschaft mbH, Cologne
Printed in Poland

ISBN 3-625-10758-9

Contents

THE IMPORTANCE OF PLANTS

Plants have an undeniable influence on our quality of life, our moods, and our well-being. It is no coincidence that we repeatedly experience nature's awakening in the spring as a new beginning: we yearn for the fresh green leaves and the first colourful blossoms that will make us forget the drabness of winter.

A classic, and still one of the most beautiful balcony plantings: a combination of ivy, pelargoniums and petunias in vivid colours.

For a long time now, people have been attempting to integrate plants into their immediate environment. They want to be surrounded by green—not only during the warm months, in the vegetation period for native plants, but all year round. With the importation of plants from the warmer regions of the earth and the construction of greenhouses, winter gardens and conservatories, this has become possible. Even the home itself has proven to be a good residence for plants. Diligent cultivation and gardening expertise have rewarded us with a huge assortment of plants that are able to flourish under widely varying conditions in our houses and flats.

Plants are fascinating, expressive elements of a person's most personal environment. A plant in a room is not a piece of furniture which unalterably claims its place and which corresponds to certain standard ideas of what a home should contain—

we are surrounded by life. The green of summer has a particularly stimulating effect that encourages all types of activity; winter's green, on the other hand, is soothing and calming.

The plants in our living rooms have long since expanded their range to include the entire home. We find houseplants and container plants everywhere: in the hallway, in the bedroom, dining room, kitchen and bathroom—and of course, on balconies and patios. In the wintertime, many plants which prefer a cooler environment at this time of year are most at home in an unheated stairwell or entryway. And we no longer keep all of our plants simply lined up on the windowsill; rather, they fill entire rooms with colour, structure, fragrance and life.

Plants let you give each room a unique look. For a particularly calming effect, leave some areas free of bright-coloured flowering plants (left).

With just a few plants and carefully selected accessories, you can conjure up a very special atmosphere. A quiet corner can even spirit you away to a favourite part of the world.

such as the living room cabinet, the couch or the kitchen counter. Rather, it provides a bit of individuality, creates change and brings a certain dynamic into the otherwise nearly static environment. It grows, it changes, it gives the room a new face. It lives, and thereby brings its environment to life.

A plant also makes different demands than a cabinet or a dresser: It wants not only to be handled, but to be cared for and looked after as well. Unlike a person or an animal, the plant remains in its place, seemingly motionless. And although it brings life into the room, it does not impose itself on anyone. Despite all the activity taking place within its organs, it radiates a beneficial calm.

Colours have an influence on a person's state of mind: Professional interior designers have been making use of this fact for some time now. Green has a calming influence; it radiates a feeling of pleasant coolness and signals that

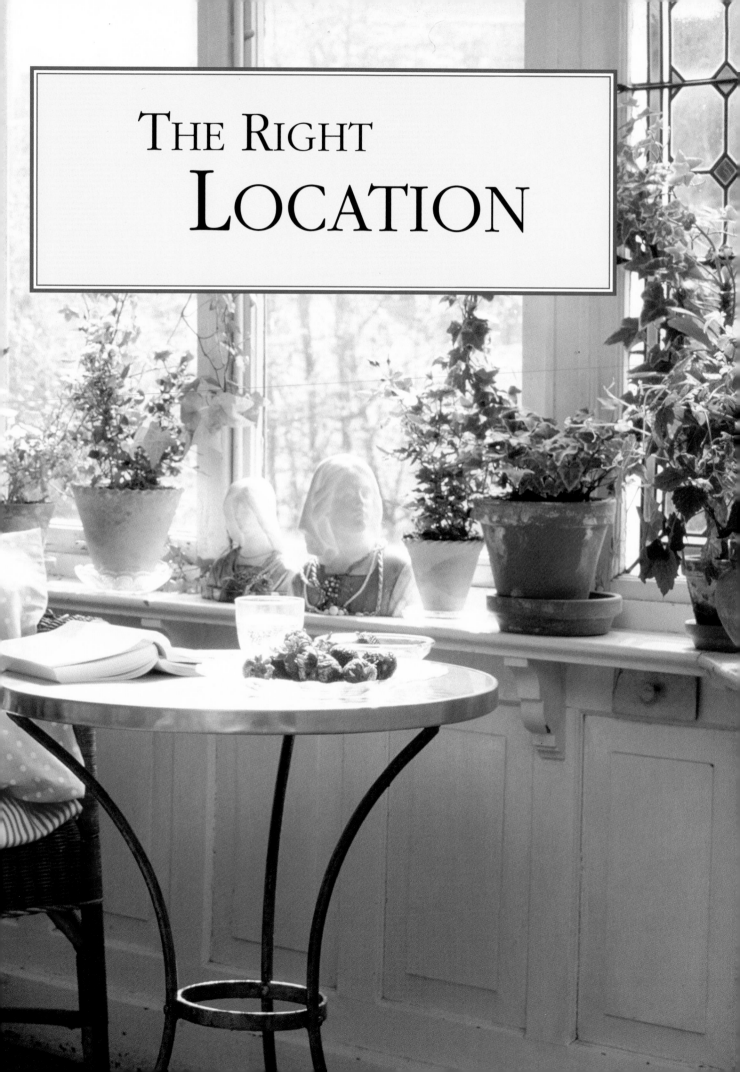

THE RIGHT
LOCATION

THE SOUTH WINDOW

Anyone who cares for houseplants in their home will have been disappointed by one or another of their green charges at some point. An originally healthy and decorative plant shrivels up, lets its leaves hang woefully, and finally dies because it has been relegated to the wrong spot in the house.

If you have a wide glass facade, you can offer your plants light conditions ranging from very bright light on the windowsill to semi-shade somewhat further back—all in a single room.

Houseplants can only reward you for the loving care you give them if they are placed in a location in which the conditions at least approximate those in their natural habitat. Naturally, most green plants—and especially most flowering plants—will find a window location to be most preferable. However, many plants do almost equally well when they are moved a little bit further into the room. Many plants which are well suited to semi-shady or even shady conditions can find an ideal home on top of a cabinet, on the dining room table, on a room divider, or even on a special flower stand somewhere within the room. The fact that houseplants have such widely varying needs with regard to light, temperature and moisture makes it possible to find an appropriate location where your green

housemates will thrive in nearly every room in the home.

The preferred orientation for living spaces is toward the south—that is, in the direction which receives the most light and the warmest rays of the sun, but which is not necessarily ideal for your green and blooming room decorations. A south window provides optimum growth conditions only for desert natives and a few heat-tested sun worshippers. But even for these plants, a little bit of shade during the hottest hours of a summer day is more beneficial than the blazing noonday sun. Many thoroughly heat-tolerant succulents require a cool location—albeit a bright one—in the winter. This holds true for most orchid cacti, including the very popular Christmas cactus.

The stars among the suitable plants for sunny south windows include the Madagascar palm, with its decorative tuft of leaves, as well as the desert rose, which craves maximum portions of warmth and sunlight, and the various types of euphorbias. Thick-leaved agaves, aloes and kalanchoes also tolerate the warmth of a sunny south window well. But even plants with opulent blossoms—such as the spectacular golden trumpet with its gleaming yellow, bell-shaped flowers—are very happy to stand in a sunny location. A particularly striking sun-lover is the thick-leaved rosary vine, whose delicate shoots drape down from a hanging pot or similar elevated location like a curtain. Some varieties of bougainvilleas also feel at home in a south window.

The kalanchoe (above) is happy with a place at a south window. Its pretty little blossoms cover a wide spectrum of colours.

Unusual combinations on the windowsill are immediate eye-catchers. Here, bougainvillea and hibiscus are next to rosemary and sage plants.

EAST AND WEST WINDOWS

The east and west sides of the house are both ideally suited as locations for house-plants—much more so than the south side with its extremely high concentration of sunlight. In these locations, plants receive abundant light from morning to evening without having to tolerate the scorching sun for many hours a day.

The east window has proven to be a particularly favourable location. This is an ideal spot for plants which love a bright but not completely sunny location. However, plants that are actually reputed to tolerate semi-shady locations can feel at home here as well. And even sun-worshipping houseplants can do very well here. On the east side of a house or flat in the early to late morning hours, the sun is not usually so powerful that shading is necessary, yet it still supplies enough light and warmth that

Typical conditions for a location at an east or west window: bright, but not completely sunny. The weeping fig is just one plant that feels at home here.

plant growth and flower development can progress steadily. At west windows, on the other hand, you may have to provide some shade on hot summer days to keep leaves and blossoms from being damaged by the excessive heat.

The list of plants that are well suited to east and west windows covers an enormous spectrum: Grandmother's African hemp stretches itself out comfortably here in the indirect sunlight, while the distinctive dracaena flourishes beautifully as well. Cyperus and weeping figs are as much at home here as many flowering plants—including African violets, impatiens, gloxinia or cyclamen. Even most orchids are well served by a location at an east or west window. Of course, you need to supply your plants with adequate—but not too much—water all year round. And remember to provide sufficient humidity—both during the hot days of summer and in winter when rooms are heated.

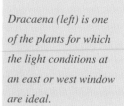

Dracaena (left) is one of the plants for which the light conditions at an east or west window are ideal.

If the position of your windows is not directly east or west but rather such that one window faces more northeast and another more northwest, it is better to decorate your windowsill with plants which, in their native lands, flourish well in a tropical rainforest. This means that while they crave a great deal of warmth, their light and sun requirements are somewhat reduced. This group of plants includes mind-your-own-business and spider plants, the popular philodendron and umbrella tree as well as various ferns; flowering plants in this category include anthurium, primroses and begonias.

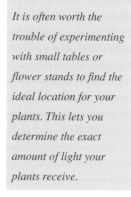

It is often worth the trouble of experimenting with small tables or flower stands to find the ideal location for your plants. This lets you determine the exact amount of light your plants receive.

While the robust yucca actually prefers a brighter location, you can achieve satisfactory results in a sheltered corner as well.

THE NORTH WINDOW

Contrary to popular opinion, the south side of the house, which receives the strongest sunshine, is not really so beneficial for the majority of plants. There are many genera and species that require a shady location, and which will flourish beautifully on a north-facing windowsill or in a darker living area.

Nevertheless, in north-facing rooms, you should be sure your plants are placed on a windowsill or on a plant stand or shelf directly in front of the window. When plants are too far from the window—that is, in the middle of the room—the lack of light will prevent their healthy development. From their perspective, it is practically night-time. Naturally, the window allowing the mild to muted northern light enter the room must not be further darkened by heavy curtains; blinds are equally unnecessary.

In addition, in dark rooms where perhaps only a little light and sunshine enter the room in the mornings and evenings—or perhaps not at all—take care not to further reduce this light by placing too many plants (especially tall ones) on the windowsill. They may do well there, but they will darken the rest of the room. A better option is to select one elegant but not too sumptuous flowering plant and place it on a flower stand whose height fits the rest of the furnishings, or to place a plant that requires less light on a sideboard or dresser, where its elegant form can beautify the whole room and not just the window alone.

Many plants are well suited to a location in a living space where the light is less favourable. The parlour palm is one thoroughly charming example; it loves indirect light and even flourishes further away from the window, ideally somewhat elevated on a flower stand or pedestal. However, the air in the room should not be too dry.

If the room where the light is less than radiantly bright is large enough, you could give a split-leaf philodendron the opportunity to spread out its massive, deeply cleft leaves. This plant, which needs to be misted frequently in summertime, can grow to a height of over 5 metres (16 ft). If you happen to have such an enormous specimen, try to keep the furniture surrounding the plant as sparse as possible so as to allow it to display all the charms of its form and structure to the fullest.

The dieffenbachia can develop its attractive leaves without making any great demands as far as light and brightness are concerned. The green varieties require less light than the white and coloured types; they can even flourish in a location further back in the room. They do not like the dry air of heated rooms, however, and should thus be misted regularly. If you're lucky, the plant will even produce flowers.

With their austere form the hard, sword-shaped leaves of the snake plant fit in well with a modern living room, especially if you have an interesting planter to place the plant in. This plant is very undemanding, and will even grow in the interior of a room. It is not sensitive to dry air, requires only moderate watering and does not suffer from a lack of light, although it prefers bright locations.

Individual plants dress up a north window while still allowing enough light to enter the room.

Even in locations that offer the most unfavourable light conditions, some plants can flourish when well cared for.

Observing the unique propagation habits of the piggy-back plant is an exciting and educational experience for any plant lover. The new little plantlets simply drop off from the leaves.

If you wish to keep houseplants in a room that lacks favourable daylight, you can take advantage of another dimension and choose hanging or climbing plants. They create a beautiful look, enlivening the room with their green leaves from an elevated location—be it a from a hanging flowerpot, a pillar, or a shelf or cabinet. For example, the Virginia creeper develops luxuriant foliage and grows satisfactorily even in semi-shady corners of the room. The same is true of the ever-popular pothos. A true expert in the art of adaptability is ivy, whose small, room-size varieties—especially the green types—are also content in relatively dark corners. However, the temperature should

not be too high in the wintertime: ivy will not do well at temperatures above 15 to 16 °C (59–61 °F). It is better, then, to place the plant in an entryway or stairwell. A particularly beautiful sight—even when seen from below—is the spider plant with its abundant green and white striped leaves and delicate blossoms. This plant also flourishes well somewhat removed from a window, and its offshoots make it very easy to propagate.

One standout among the green plants that tolerate shade well is the piggyback plant, also called youth-on-age or mother-of-thousands, which looks especially nice in a hanging pot. It produces its offspring directly out of its

There are also a number of flowering house-plants which will develop a lovely abundance of blossoms even in less bright locations. In addition to the extremely popular African violet, which will bloom very well even on a dining room table or a sideboard, there are such delightful varieties as mondo grass. This member of the lily family not only has long, grass-like leaves, but also develops delicate, hanging flower buds in the summertime. Plants with green foliage do better in not-so-bright living spaces than those whose leaves have light-coloured stripes. These plants should be misted frequently, and it is very important that mondo grass spend the winter in an unheated room.

Even when placed 2 to 3 metres (6–10 ft) away from a window, the peace lily will produce its large, flower-like white spathes from amid its luxuriant green foliage. This plant, which is also excellently suited to hydroponic culture, looks very decorative when placed at a somewhat elevated location.

leaves. The young plantlets simply fall off when they have reached maturity. This plant requires a great deal of fresh air. It prefers to be cool in the wintertime, so it is best to move it into the stairwell.

Some ferns look particularly striking in elevated locations, but are also attractive in hanging pots. However, the staghorn fern, with its bizarrely shaped leaves, should not be placed too far away from a source of light. On the other hand, polypody can also make do with less light—but just like the interesting hart's tongue fern, it is happier in a cooler location in the wintertime (10–12 °C/50–54 °F).

Boston ferns and Virginia creepers (left) look best when placed in a somewhat elevated location from which their abundant tendrils can spill down unhindered.

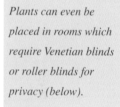

Plants can even be placed in rooms which require Venetian blinds or roller blinds for privacy (below).

17

LIGHT CONDITIONS

The larger the living space, the more possibilities are available for attractive and individual decoration with plants. If you also have a large glass facade, or windows on two sides of the room which allow the light to stream in unhindered, you can give nearly free rein to your decorating wishes.

Wonderful locations for plants can be found in every home. This pothos looks particularly elegant against a white wall.

Before you get started decorating a room with plants, you should keep in mind that the light directly adjacent to a window is very muted—especially when the window is also covered with curtains or drapes—even if this fact might not be evident at first glance.

Therefore, the plants most suitable for placing to the right and left sides of the windows in a bright dining room or living room are not those that need sun, but those which flourish in semi-shady areas—for example, a Boston fern on a pedestal, or an umbrella tree with its beautifully shaped leaves. However, you could also place a whole basket filled with African violet plants as an eye-catcher in a less favourably lit spot.

It is important to note that brightness decreases very quickly as you move toward the interior of a room. Thus, you should not place plants which require sunny locations or bright indirect light at any distance from the windows. For this reason, you should never place a blooming gloxinia or primrose on the dining room table or coffee table. The same is true for passion flowers or kalanchoes—as delightful as they all may appear in these locations. Over the long term, they would suffer from the constant lack of light. Less light-hungry plants—which are therefore better suited to a spot on a dresser somewhat removed from the window, or on the dining room table—are the previously mentioned African violets or the common primrose.

If you are have fantastic specimens such as these (above left), use carefully selected planters to create just the right overall impression.

Some people like sumptuous blossoms, while others prefer a more reserved focus on the pure essentials (above right).

The split-leaf philodendron is nearly unstoppable in its growth. It displays its splendour most beautifully when allowed to stand alone.

If sufficiently wide windowsills are not available, the most luxuriously growing houseplants can find a home somewhere else in the room. They look particularly decorative placed next to an especially attractive piece of furniture, an unusual lamp, in front of a white wall or accompanied by other room decorations. Their beautiful form or structure is especially eye-catching in an exposed location. But as soon as the giants among the houseplants are moved more than 1 to 2 metres (3–6 ft) away from a window, you must make certain they can tolerate shade.

Large plants which require a great deal of light include the African hemp, members of the rubber tree family, the false aralia, the sago palm and the radermachera. These varieties should be placed at or in front of a window with as much space around them as possible.

Among the large plants that tolerate shade well are the Kentia palm—which can grow to several metres in height—kangaroo vines or grape ivy, the parlour palm and the split-leaf philodendron with its characteristic huge leaves. Dracaena can also work its way up to impressive heights, and it tolerates moderate shade.

When any of these plants—which are practically indoor trees—reaches the limit imposed by the ceiling or a piece of furniture, it is often possible to take your garden shears in hand and prune the plant back. The African hemp, for example, tolerates pruning without complaint; you can use the cut-off shoots to cultivate new plants if you like. You can also take shears to the branches of a split-leaf philodendron or a radermachera—a beautiful foliage plant which has its origins in China. In the case of tall-growing palms, however, pruning is not the proper solution for overgrowth. Here, you need to prepare ahead of time by keeping the plant's container relatively small, even when re-potting, and providing the roots with some support.

As much as green and blooming houseplants improve the quality of life in your living space, you should not simply distribute as many plants as possible along your windowsills and in the room itself: Less can sometimes be more. An especially decorative foliage plant requires sufficient space to display itself to its full advantage. Likewise, a plant with attractive blossoms can best work its magic when it stands alone. This is true, for example, of such elegant beauties as the gardenia. Other varieties, such as primroses or African violets, only reveal the full extent of their charms when displayed in a group. However, it is not only the overall impression that suffers when there are too many plants in a room: the well-being of the plants is affected as well, and the great abundance could quickly become a burden for the plant lover.

Like many other robust larger plants, the ficus can easily tolerate radical pruning when it threatens to grow too large for its location.

PLANTS IN THE BEDROOM AND BATHROOM

For a long time, people believed that bedrooms had to be kept free of plants. But in fact, the amount of oxygen they require during the night is not a problem as long as only a few plants grace your bedroom; the strong fragrance of some flowering plants is the only potential disturbance. On the other hand, foliage plants provide a room with oxygen all day long. The bathroom is also a relatively new discovery as a location for houseplants.

> Anyone who loves plants will not want to do without their simultaneously calming and stimulating effects. However, to ensure restful sleep with sufficient oxygen, you should limit the number of plants in your bedroom.

The climate in the bedroom suits the needs of many plants, since it is often kept relatively cool in the winter and is likely to face east or northeast. A weeping fig, for example, feels right at home near a window and brings a pleasant, light green colour into the boudoir. The delicate creeping fig with its long hanging shoots could also look delightful on a high pedestal. If your bedroom faces north, so that little light enters through the window, shade-loving plants such as a luxuriant fern or a pothos are good choices. Cyperus will bring more moisture into the room, as well as a touch of exotic, far-Eastern charm. This plant prefers to be close to the window, and should always have water in its saucer. Fragrant flowering plants, on the other hand, definitely do not belong in the bedroom.

Sleeping in a room with plants is not recommended for people with allergies. They react

not only to flower pollens, but in some cases to spores and moulds which may develop on the soil or on the clay pellets of hydroponic plants. As a general rule, the room should be decorated only with a single plant.

Bathrooms, with their relatively high temperature and humidity, are clearly not the best location for every flowering or foliage plant. However, some varieties native to tropical realms will be in their element under these conditions. Here are just a few plants which feel at home in a bathroom environment: for locations somewhat removed from the window, the maidenhair fern, with its pretty green fronds, is a good choice. It does not like to be cooler than 18 °C (64 °F), and even in winter it prefers temperatures from 20 to 22 °C (68–72 °F). The pothos also requires warmth: In the summer it is content with temperatures from 17 to 20 °C (63–68 °F); in winter, it needs to be kept between 20 and 24 °C (68–75 °F). If you're looking for something exclusive, place a lady's slipper orchid in a somewhat dimly lit bathroom. This plant likes temperatures starting at 17 °C (63 °F) in the summer, and develops well between 18 and 22 °C (64–72 °F) in the winter. The lovely, two-coloured rex begonia vine can be an eye-catcher in the bathroom.

Providing it with temperatures starting at 18 to 20 °C (64–68 °F) in the summer should be no problem; in the winter it tolerates temperatures between 15 and 25 °C (59–77 °F). It prefers an elevated location close to a window. In a bright spot the bird's nest fern produces wide, beautiful leaves, but the room temperature should not be much above 20 °C (68 °F) in winter.

PLANTS IN THE KITCHEN AND HALLWAY

Nowadays, many kitchens are not much more than an alcove in which every last bit of space is put to use. Nevertheless, if you have a window of any size, you shouldn't deny yourself a view of rich green foliage even here. Spacious hallways, entryways or stairways are also by no means taboo as locations for houseplants, either—even when they offer relatively little light.

Kitchen surfaces generally need to be kept clear for work. But up on a shelf, plants will not disturb even complicated preparations.

In addition to the tiny kitchens mentioned above, the trend today is back toward kitchens which can be cooking, eating and living space all at once. In this type of kitchen-cum-living room, there is always a place for plants. Which plants can best tolerate the alternating atmosphere of heat from cooking and baking combined with drafts from airing the room? It's worth trying out a filigreed bulrush, which does not grow overly large and whose thin, delicate leaves hang downward: It requires a semi-shady location, generous watering and constant humidity. Cyperus, with its high water consumption, is quite content in the kitchen, provided you have enough space near a window for this fast-growing plant. Pothos is also happy to creep downward from a somewhat elevated spot such as a kitchen cabinet or shelf; it is also content with a location that is not quite so bright.

Of course, edible green things are particularly desirable in the kitchen. You can keep an entire potted garden of cooking herbs on a shelf you install yourself near a window.

Plants in the entryway or stairwell offer a friendly welcome to anyone entering the house. Naturally, in this somewhat shady environment, only plants which do not require a large amount of light will do well. Since temperatures in these areas are also lower than in your living space, the number of appropriate plants is limited still further.

One possibility is the nearly indestructible spider plant, whose slender, pale-green leaves can bring a friendly brightness into the entryway. Pothos is also quite shade-tolerant and looks delightful in a hanging pot. The severe snake plant is satisfied with a medium-bright

location in an entryway or stairwell, as is the undemanding cast iron plant, which has already been gracing entryways for generations, it seems. The Japanese aralia prefers to spend the summer in a shady place outdoors, but in the wintertime it also looks very decorative in a cool stairwell or entryway with its shiny, lobed leaves. Tradescantia, with its hanging shoots and its pretty, usually striped leaves, is very modest in its demands for light. If you have room for a hanging pot or a fairly high shelf, you should place one of these luxuriantly growing plants in your hallway or entryway. The asparagus fern is a charming sight that can enliven an otherwise dreary entryway or hallway; it willingly sends out its shoots, even in a semi-shady location. In short, all of these locations are well suited to any of those plants which prefer a cool place in the wintertime.

Since the philodendron (left) is not sensitive to many things except direct sunlight, it is a good plant to place in a stairwell.

In a somewhat roomier entryway, the giant proportions of the split-leaf philodendron is exactly the right choice. It creates an attractive transition to the next floor of the house.

Placing potted herbs among the flowers creates a welcome connection between the decorative and the useful—and the effect is definitely Mediterranean.

PLANTS FOR PATIOS AND BALCONIES

A balcony or patio allows you to fulfil nearly all your dreams of a green—or more accurately, a colourful—oasis and to demonstrate your individuality in a very small space. Until just a few years ago, the key word "balcony" made most people think of geraniums; nowadays, an enormous selection of plants is available to encourage you in your urge to experiment.

The limited space of a patio, terrace or balcony does have its advantages, and the restrictions it places on your choice of plants presents a new challenge every year. If you wish to create a consistent atmosphere with your plantings, you need to plan ahead. Perennial plants should receive first considera- tion: which of your existing container plants can be moved out of their winter quarters and into the open, and when? Where will they be placed? How much space do they need? What colourful accents do they bring to the space? And conversely, which of your houseplants will enjoy the fresh summer air on the patio? You can then create groupings around these leading players according to your moods or desires—always keeping light requirements in mind. Purists select their plantings all in one colour, or in varying tones of the same plant species. Other gardeners create a colourful new "clutter" every year, making use of every last bit of space—even on the walls or hanging from above. This type of patio contains everything from a herb corner to a container filled with tomatoes or wild strawberries.

Planting your patio in a certain regional character also creates a lovely effect—for example, a Mediterranean look with bougainvillea, miniature orange trees and oleander. Corresponding balcony furniture, flowerpots typical of the country and other accessories will further contribute to conjuring up a holiday atmosphere in an everyday place.

In planning your patio or balcony, it's very important to consider the order in which the various plants will blossom. This small work of art will only be a true success if from spring to autumn there is always something new to admire. The first daffodils and hyacinths will naturally set the mood for the lighter season; pelargoniums or petunias show their brilliance in the summertime; and in autumn, heather and chrysanthemums take centre stage in the play of colour.

However, even holiday dreams need to be considered carefully. Most patio plants require intensive care. Particularly in midsummer, daily watering is a must; in the case of some particularly thirsty species, such as petunias or angel's trumpets, you will have to water twice a day. If you are frequently away from home, special watering systems are recommended. In addition, careful removal of faded blossoms is as important as regular watering if you wish to enjoy a long-lasting abundance of flowers.

A balcony can radiate with beautiful colour nearly year round. In the autumn, chrysanthemums and Boston ivy playfully take on this task.

By making clever use of every dimension, you can turn your balcony into a summery oasis. You can then happily postpone your holidays until the winter months.

POTS, BOXES AND CONTAINERS

Even a person who doesn't believe that they have a green thumb can make a completely stress-free attempt at gardening on the patio. Beginners need not invest in expensive perennials, but can stick with reliable annuals—any mistakes made will not result in major damage. The nice thing is, next year everything can look completely different.

Balcony and patio gardening is the perfect way to a feel for what plants need. In the first year, you can simply select the hardiest varieties: You can't go far wrong with marigolds, geraniums or petunias. These plants are also an especially good choice for households with children. You can easily entrust the little ones to take care of them, and they will soon be competing to see whose plants are blooming most beautifully. It is also extremely fascinating for young and old alike to observe the way the entire life cycle of a plant takes place over a period of just a few months: from the planting of seeds or seedlings in the spring through abundant blossoming in the summer, to fading and dying off in the autumn. Experience shows that beginners tend to underestimate the size of individual flowers and to plant them much too close together. As a general rule of thumb, you can follow these guidelines: Plant smaller plants such as marigolds or verbena approximately

> Imposing container plants should only be grouped together in rare cases. When given sufficient space, the oleander becomes a true eye-catcher.

Planted a bit too close and jumbled all together, pelargoniums, fuchsia, impatiens and lobelia exude a joyful summer atmosphere.

15 cm (6 in) apart; larger varieties such as pelargoniums or petunias need to be at least 20 to 30 cm (8–12 in) away from each other. Another typical beginners' mistake is to be much too timid about pruning. Many plants which are nearing the end of their first bloom-ing period in the summertime can frequently be prompted to blossom a second time if you cut back their main shoots almost to the halfway point. However, this does not hold true for plants which bloom continuously up through October—here you should only remove faded or wilted blossoms.

If your first season was a success, you can turn to more difficult subjects. These include, for example, plantings in shady corners—for which impatiens, begonias or fuchsias are appropriate choices. The most impor-tant thing here is to avoid over-watering so as not to rot the roots. Caring for perennials is also an interesting task. If you have some im-pressive specimens in containers, you can give your patio a new face every year by reposition-ing the plants. A "fragrance balcony" is anoth-er exciting option. The point here is to combine plants according to fragrances which comple-ment one another but which should not become bothersome. Scented pelargoniums, in particu-lar, are well worth discovering in this context.

Fuchsias (left) are a traditional balcony or patio plant. They are well suited to shady or semi-shady corners.

THE PROPER
CARE

PLANT CONTAINERS IN SUMMER AND WINTER

If you want to treat your plants well and enjoy them for a long time, you will create the proper starting conditions for them. We have already discussed the importance of light and its influence on your choice of locations. Equally important is the attention paid to temperature and humidity, as well as the containers in which your plants are housed.

Efflorescence—the appearance of lime and salt deposits on the outer surface of clay pots—is not harmful to the plant, but diminishes the visual impression.

For most houseplants, the summer months pose no problems. The heat and humidity are comfortable for the majority of plants. It is important, however, to ensure that the humidity in your living space is adequate in the cold part of the year. After all, many houseplants are native to tropical rainforests and are therefore accustomed to moist air as well as to sufficient warmth. When the air is dry from artificial heating, plants need to be misted regularly.

Air supply is another factor to consider. Windows are generally kept open in the summertime; however, houseplants require fresh air in the wintertime as well. Ventilation is important, even in rainy, snowy or cold weather—but naturally, you should never expose your plants to drafts or to any sudden icy blasts.

Countless houseplants are capable of spending the summer on a wind-protected balcony or on the patio without any problems. It goes without saying that oleander, agaves, yucca and pelargoniums will leave their winter homes by mid-May, at the latest, and move out into the fresh air. But palms, ivies, cacti and even African hemp will also welcome the outdoors in summer; it is simply important to protect them from drafts and wind.

The flowerpots, dishes, containers and boxes which take the place of a natural flower bed for your plants should not only look attractive and show the plants off to their best advantage, they are also an important element of plant care. After all, they not only serve the purpose of providing your plants with stability and support, but the plants must also be able to survive, grow—and in some cases even blossom and bear fruit—in these vessels under less than ideal conditions.

Potting options include traditional clay pots, hard plastic containers and the newer pots and dishes made of environmentally friendly, biodegradable material.

Thanks to their weight, clay pots are quite stable; the material is somewhat porous and, to a certain degree, permeable to water, nutrients and oxygen. In addition to the risk of breakage, with extended use, clay pots also have an aesthetic flaw in that they develop "efflorescence". Lime and salts work their way through the porous clay and appear as unattractive stains on the outer surface.

Plastic pots are longer lasting, since they are fairly resistant to breakage and are cheaper to manufacture. The substrate inside them is generally warmer and roots spread through them more evenly. Since plastic pots have no decorative value and are also unstable for plants with a great deal of foliage, they are usually placed inside planters.

Especially during the season when your home is heated, many plants are extremely grateful for a regular misting with water.

When ferns are allowed to spend the summer out-of-doors, you can place nearly anything beside them: the result will always be a romantic still life.

Press the plant firmly into the new substrate. The pot should not be filled to the brim; on average, you can figure on allowing about 2 cm (³/₄ in) of watering space.

THE RIGHT SOIL

The composition of the soil is critically important to your houseplants' well-being. Many unsuccessful attempts at container cultivation can be traced back to inadequate soil conditions. When the quality of the soil is poor, one negative reaction can trigger the next. In such cases, re-potting is often the only way to save the plant.

Every substrate must possess certain qualities, without which the plants' roots would not be able to serve their purpose—that is, to absorb water and nutrients. A good potting soil should be nutritious, light and warm, as well as porous and water permeable, thus allowing the roots to obtain oxygen. On the other hand, the substrate must be capable of bonding with water, in order that water and nutrients do not simply flow past the roots.

So-called standard potting soils as well as industrially produced soils are preferable to mixtures of soil and compost taken from your own garden. They have been developed especially as

you should never re-pot your plants is the vegetation period in the wintertime, when the plants' growth appears to have come to a complete standstill. You should not disturb your plants when they are in this state, since re-potting a plant encourages new activity. Of course, you should also refrain from re-potting your plants while they are in full bloom.

A good rule of thumb is to re-pot small and medium-sized houseplants in fresh potting soil every year, and large plants every two to three years. In addition, you can recognise that a plant urgently needs to be re-potted if the surface of the substrate is crusted over or even mossy, or if the roots are already growing out of the drainage holes. When this occurs, it is definitely high time to move your plant to a more comfortable container and offer its root system more space.

Be they clay or plastic, the variety of plant containers available in all sizes is impressive; you can find the perfect pot for any plant (left).

Extremely dense root development can be seen on this kaffir lily (below). A plant in this condition, needs to be immediately re-potted in a significantly larger container.

potting soils, are hygienically safe and the quality is uniform. Standard potting soil consists of 60–80 % white peat and 20–40 % clay as well as lime and additional nutrients. In recent years, as the moors have become increasingly endangered by peat harvesting, bark products are also being added more and more frequently. Standard potting soil is available in two forms: the heavily fertilised type that is suitable for the majority of houseplants and a type to which less fertiliser has been added, appropriate for the cultivation of young plants (called cultivation soil) and for salt-sensitive varieties such as bromeliads or palms. A peat growth medium/potting compost (TKS) has similar properties to a standard potting soil; however, it retains a great deal of water. Mixtures of potting soil and peat growth media have proven to be very effective as well. Peat growth media are also available in two different forms—one with a smaller addition of fertiliser (TKS 1) and one with a greater addition (TKS 2). Consult a salesperson when purchasing a medium.

The composition of the soil in a plant pot changes over time; it becomes worn out. The nutrient content is eventually exhausted, and frequent watering and fertilising lead to acidification of the soil. Now is the time to renew the soil—in other words, to re-pot the plant, ideally in the spring. The only time of year

PRECISION WATERING AND FERTILISING

How much and how often you need to water varies from one plant to the next. (For specifics see individual plant descriptions in the compendium.) What is important is that the substrate—the soil in the pot—is thoroughly moistened but not wet. After all, it is possible to have too much of a good thing. In the case of fertiliser, as well, less is often more.

The most important prerequisite for helping a plant to flourish is regular watering, tailored to the plant's individual needs.

It is best to water only when the surface of the soil feels dry. Watering regularly but sparingly is better than over-watering at irregular intervals. You can then assume that the entire root ball is moistened. Surprisingly enough, more plants die from excess watering than from being overly dry. Therefore, it is less dangerous to wait an extra day to water your plants than it is to drown them. However, if the ball of soil has become completely dry—for example, if you have been away from home for a long time—the best method is to submerge the entire plant in a pail of water, leaving it in until no more air bubbles rise to the surface. Some plants find an occasional dip extremely pleasant even if they were not dried out beforehand. The water that your plants receive from the watering can should never be too

cold. This is particularly important in the wintertime, when they are especially sensitive to any cold shock. You should therefore fill the watering can several hours before watering and wait until the water has warmed to room temperature.

When is it best to fertilise? The rule here is that plants require the most nutrients during the growing period and when producing flowers, which generally begins in the spring and ends in the autumn. The exceptions, of course, are those plants which reveal the glory of their blossoms in the wintertime—for example, Christmas cactus, cyclamen and azaleas.

However, if you have re-potted plants early in the spring—when the first growth spurt begins for the majority of plants—you can postpone your first round of fertilising for a few weeks, since the fresh potting soil will contain the necessary nutrients in the proper concentrations. Later on, follow the manufacturer's dosage recommendations. This generally means your plants will get all the nutrients they need if fertilised at 1 to 2-week intervals. You won't do your plants a favour by overdosing them with fertiliser or fertilising them more often. Keep in mind, as well, that plants kept in particularly dark locations require much less fertiliser, or perhaps none at all.

Over-fertilising is more harmful to most plants than a temporary low supply of nutrients. Thus, if you try to help a weak plant "get back on its feet" with an extra portion of fertiliser, your kind intentions will not benefit the plant at all. In fact, "needy children" like this should be fertilised very sparingly, if at all. Instead you should increase the dosage only when the plant begins to get stronger again. If the plant cannot absorb the fertiliser, salt deposits will accumulate in the pot, which can lead to root damage.

In addition to liquid fertilisers, powdered forms which are spread over the substrate are also available (above).

If the substrate becomes totally dried out, you can often rescue a plant by immersing it completely in a pail of water (opposite page, bottom).

Fertiliser sticks (left), which release their ingredients steadily over a longer period of time are a practical option.

GIVING SHAPE TO YOUR PLANTS

Some older plants become gawky-looking over time—leggy and bare at the bottom with a sickly appearance—however, many of them can be pruned quite easily. If you wish to give your plants a different shape, you will need to make a training cut at the proper time. And if you want them to climb upwards in a lovely form, they will need an appropriate support.

Portable climbing screens can easily assume the role of room dividers and thus create defined spaces within a larger area.

Some of the most beautiful flowering plants can be stimulated to produce abundant blossoms by means of a radical, rejuvenating trim. A bougainvillea will tolerate this procedure just as well as a hibiscus or a noble passion flower, an azalea or a flowering maple. All these plants will repay you for the pruning job with more beautiful blooms in the coming vegetation period. The prerequisite for successful pruning is a good—and above all, a clean—tool to work with. For cutting tender shoots you will need a sharp knife; woody branches require a pair of garden shears. It is important to cut just above a leaf joint and to ensure that the cut is smooth; messy cuts will damage the shoot. In fleshy plants, some liquid will seep out at the cutting point—the plant bleeds. If this occurs, simply spray a little water over the cut. If you cut back a very thick branch or stem, leaving a

A less radical technique than pruning is pinching back. This involves simply pinching off the soft, young tips of the shoots with your fingernails in order to stimulate the plant to branch out further and produce fuller growth. You can also increase the blooming potential of many flowering plants in this way.

Climbing plants that grow in containers require supports in order to grow up the side of a wall or fence. Self-climbing plants need support only at the beginning of their growth. They later develop various methods of clinging to walls by themselves. Other plants, which do not develop these abilities, need to be attached at the desired location, and new shoots must also be secured regularly.

There are many different kinds of supports to choose from. Bamboo poles work very well for short-lived plants; you can easily tie them together to create a kind of network or form a trellis out of them using strings. Rings and clips are good methods for securing a wire along a wall. They allow for good air circulation and thus reduce the possibility of attacks by pests.

large cut exposed, it is best to rub some charcoal powder onto the surface of the cut.

The degree to which a plant should be pruned depends on the type of plant in question as well as on the specific features of that particular plant. A rubber tree which only has a few leaves remaining at the top of a 1-metre (3-ft) stem should be pruned back to 12 to 15 cm (5–6 in) above the edge of the pot. New leaves will soon grow out of the remaining stem. You should water the plant only sparingly after such a pruning, since the leaf mass, which consumes the lion's share of the water, is now greatly reduced.

Climbing plant supports provide an attractive way of protecting your privacy if you also use them for the upper section of thickly growing plants such as knotweed (left).

Cutting back at the right spot will stimulate almost any plant to vigorous growth. You can achieve an entirely new shape by making quite radical training cuts (below).

HYDROPONICS

Many plant lovers would like to have blooming houseplants on their windowsills, or long for something fresh and green in their homes, especially during the winter months. However, they may have too little time to care for flowering plants, shy away from providing the constant care that plants require, or travel frequently. All these people are good candidates for hydroponics: indoor gardening with a minimum of effort.

This is still a relatively unusual sight, but hydro-ponic culture is in fact suitable even for container plants that are placed outdoors.

This form of cultivation—in which foliage plants as well as food plants are kept in containers filled with nutrient solutions—is a very convenient, modern system for the indoor gardener. Frequent watering and fertilising are not necessary, making this type of plant care increasingly popular.

The knowledge of plant nutrition that underlies hydroponics is not new; nutrient solutions have used for a long time in research situations. In hydroponics, plants do not anchor their roots in soil as a delivery system for nutrients; rather, they grow in containers loosely filled with a substrate of clay granules (expanded clay). This provides stability and allows the organs that supply the plant to be in contact with the nutrient solutions and air.

Expanded clay is a foamy, porous insulation material originally used in construction. The expanded clay substrate that is specially processed for hydroponics is burned from low-salt clay. It is odourless and chemically neutral; it doesn't decay or rot, is very lightweight and retains a certain amount of moisture which it slowly releases, increasing the humidity of the surrounding air. A water level meter keeps track of the amount of water or nutrient solution in the pot. The plant will only do well if the level is not too high for extended periods of time. On the other hand, constant dryness—that is, a low water level—can be equally damaging. It is best to maintain the water level at the "minimum" mark—or ideally at "optimum". You should only fill the container to the "maximum" level if you will be absent for some time. In order to maintain its reliability,

you will need to clean the water level meter periodically to keep it free of ingrown roots, fertiliser residue and dirt.

The location of the plants in the room as well as the light intensity and temperature in that location also play a crucial role in hydroponic plant care. The widely held belief that hydroponically cultivated plants require less light than other potted plants is simply false.

In terms of propagation methods—that is, cultivating young plants either from cuttings or from seeds—there is no fundamental difference between hydroponics and soil cultivation. Theoretically, it is possible to transfer a plant from soil to hydroponic culture. However, the process is somewhat laborious and not always successful.

In principle, any plant can be grown hydroponically. Since this method requires minimal care and effort it is becoming increasingly popular (left).

The basic tools of hydroponics: plant containers, expanded clay substrate and a water level meter (below).

CONTAINER PLANTS IN WINTER

In the spring and summer, plant lovers enjoy decorating their balconies, patios and gardens with a wide variety of container plants. However, they often overlook the fact that many of these plants—unlike annual flowers—need to be protected from frost in the wintertime, which is not always a simple task.

Many container plants require a rest period in the wintertime, for which the average temperatures inside the house would be too high. In addition, most perennial, shrub-like plants do not look particularly attractive when they lose their leaves and their stalks become wilted—they do not make very good room decorations. One happy exception is tuberous plants such as begonias. Depending on the variety, they can bloom well long into autumn if they are brought indoors and treated like houseplants. When their blooming season is finally over, the below-ground sections of the plant should be allowed to dry and stored in dry peat for the winter months.

When given special care, pelargoniums (as geraniums are called, using correct botanical terminology) can also survive over the winter: you can either store them or hang them up. Dig

> If there's no alternative home for your plant during winter, you can wrap a plant container in plastic film or bags to protect it from frost.

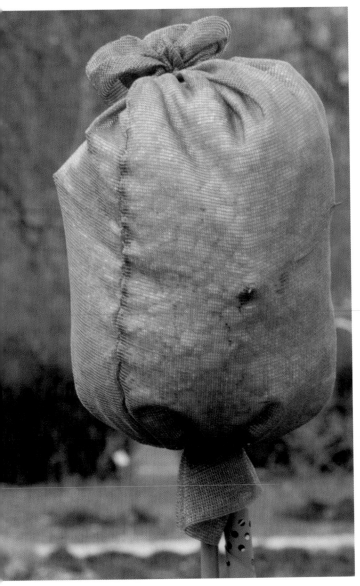

the plants up before the first frost, shake off any excess soil, and prune the plants back to a height of about 20 cm (8 in). Cut the stems exactly at the axils in order to avoid stumps of dying stems which could become susceptible to disease. Place the pruned plants in wooden boxes that contain moist peat, making sure that there is enough peat to ensure the plants are separated from one another. Store the boxes in a cool but frost-free location. Alternatively, you can hang the plants upside down in the same environment.

Another method is to remove the excess soil from the roots and wrap the dry plants in newspaper. These plant "packages" can then be placed in a wooden box and stored in a cool, dark, frost-free room. In the early spring, or whenever the danger of frost has passed in your area, you can bring the plants out of storage. Remove any dead sections or long, colourless shoots before re-potting.

If no storage space is available, many shrubs and climbing plants can survive the winter out-of-doors—with your help and a little bit of luck. Any valuable plants that you definitely don't want to lose should be covered for protection. There are special coconut and raffia mats available for this purpose; however, bubble wrap, pine twigs and piled leaves will also work well. Make sure the top of the shrub is protected, even if you damage a few of the upper branches in the process. You should also take care to see that the plant can breathe under its protective covering and that no fungi are developing. Another option is to cover your plants with sacks (not plastic); flowerpots may be covered completely.

High-stemmed plants can be protected for the winter by wrapping the top of the plant in sacks (left).

Very large plants can be moved to winter quarters with the right equipment: hand-carts are practical for this purpose (right).

DISEASES AND PESTS

It is not surprising that houseplants are sensitive. First of all, the majority of the plants which we keep indoors originated in areas of the world where the climate is completely different than ours. In addition, we force them to live in spaces that are pleasant and comfortable for us as human beings, but not necessarily for the plants. The limited space in which we allow plants' root systems to develop is yet another factor.

Generations of growers have attempted to train their plants to be less susceptible to illness or damage and more adaptable to their environment. Nevertheless, they remain delicate creatures which often react sensitively to neglect, mistakes made in caring for them or harmful environmental influences; they begin to shrivel up, become sick and even die.

The majority of houseplant problems can be traced to a wrong location or improper care— this also applies to fungal diseases and insect infestations. Healthy, robust plants rarely become diseased: the patients are almost exclusively houseplants which were already weakened or were ill at the time of purchase. Thus, houseplant diseases and pests occur as a reaction to unfavourable conditions.

The most common mistakes made in caring for plants include the following:

- An inappropriate location that is too bright or too dark for the plant

> Mechanical defence is the first step in combating pests. You can remove pests either by wiping down the leaves or by rinsing them off.

- Temperatures too warm or too cold
- Watering too infrequently or too frequently, or with water that is too cold
- Insufficient humidity for certain plants, particularly in centrally heated rooms in winter
- Drafts, or too little fresh air
- Inappropriate or inadequate substrate
- Failure to re-pot
- Failure to reduce temperatures during the plant's rest period

Before you resort to chemicals to combat fungal diseases or harmful insects, you should first exhaust other means of undoing the damage. Move the plants to a location with more appropriate temperature or light conditions; change your watering habits; possibly replace the substrate or remove pests by mechanical means. Even biological methods of pest removal are possible for houseplants in some cases.

If neither mechanical defence nor other methods prove helpful — there are a wide variety of traditional home remedies as well as new, experimental approaches — you may have to turn to chemicals. There are times when even the most environmentally conscious indoor gardener has no other choice. If you must work with poisonous substances, do so on a balcony or patio or in the garden — or at the very least with the windows open. But even if you are temporarily successful using chemical substances, it is important to realise that these methods will only remove the results of the problem — the causes still remain. The correct approach is to remove the sources of the illness or infestation.

Here, it is obvious that the plant's pot was much too small. Plants forced to live under such unfavourable conditions have little defence against diseases or pests.

A proven method for combating pests is the use of these yellow, glue-coated strips.

Many diseases can be prevented through careful maintenance, including occasionally cleaning the plant's leaves (above).

Take particular care to isolate any plants which have become infested (right).

Unlike viruses and bacteria, parasitic fungi can attack plants even without the help of carriers. With few exceptions, a warm, moist climate is the most favourable one for the development of fungal diseases, or mycoses. Houseplants are most at risk in areas where they are placed very close together and where the air circulation is poor. Weakened growth and excessive fertiliser (particularly nitrogen) can also make plants susceptible to fungi. Mycoses can affect every part of the plant: there are root diseases, branch rot, leaf and vascular diseases, and fungal damage to stems and twigs. Each of these diseases requires special treatment. In the case of a severe attack, you will have to discard the plant; when a disease is still at its onset, you can remove the affected sections and treat the rest of the plant prophylactically. It is essential to keep the plant isolated.

The most common diseases:

■ Powdery mildew — Powdery mildew can be identified by a white coating which it is possible to wipe off. It appears especially on the surfaces of the leaves, but may also

Bacteria can only enter a plant through damaged areas or natural cracks or fissures, and — just as in the case of viruses — insects (particularly aphids), or even the gardeners themselves, are most often the carriers. Attacks are aided and abetted by warmth and high humidity. Symptoms of bacterial disease include cancer-like growths on a plants roots or stalks (e.g., in oleander), wilting and decaying branches (more common in pelargoniums) or oily spots in the case of begonias. Unfortunately, it is not possible to combat bacterial diseases or to heal them using pesticides. In order to avoid infecting your other plants, you must separate the diseased plants immediately and throw them in the rubbish bin.

Viral diseases are also caused by microscopic agents; viruses enter the plant's body through open wounds. They are passed on to houseplants in the same way as bacteria.

Affected plants (such as chrysanthemums, dahlias or lilies) will develop mottled yellow leaves which finally wilt. The plant's shoots may turn reddish or the plant's growth may become stunted. Viral diseases in plants are also incurable: any diseased plants belong in the bin.

be found on buds, shoots or in some cases, on blossoms.

■ Downy mildew or pseudo mildew—Typical signs of downy mildew are a greyish-white, fuzzy mould on the surface of the leaves, with brown spots on the underside.

■ Parasitic rust disease—This fungus can be recognised by the yellow, rust-brown, or sometimes orange coloured pustules—the summer spore pods—on the undersides of the leaves. When these become rampant the leaves shrivel up and wilt, and the plant eventually dies.

■ Grey rot or botrytis blight—This common harmful mould can also affect potted plants. The external symptoms appear as a greyish-brown, fuzzy mould; later on, slimy, rotting blotches appear on the leaves.

The root ball of a plant can be affected by a variety of pests—for example, wood lice. It is often helpful to remove the plant from the pot and allow the substrate to dry out.

A frequently asked question among beginning indoor gardeners is how pests can appear on their carefully tended plants from one day to the next. Indeed, even the most seasoned houseplant lover who works with disinfected soil, scrupulously clean tools, etc., will still occasionally be surprised by an apparent assault of entire hordes of aphids, mealybugs or spider mites and will ask him or herself where these pests could have come from so suddenly.

The clichéd expression "out of thin air" may sound meaningless, but in fact, it is not wrong. Like bacteria, viruses and fungus spores, insect pests can literally come out of the air. Roundworms in flowerpots may have been brought in with the soil, since their eggs can often survive exposure to high temperatures—even disinfection processes.

Here is a detailed list of the unwelcome intruders that may visit a houseplant paradise:

- Ants—Ants often appear during an attack of aphids, since they are attracted to the "honeydew" that the latter secrete. They will normally disappear again once the aphids have been successfully removed.

- Lice—These small, slate-coloured to yellowish grey, crablike creatures like to feed on the fleshy sections of plants during the night.

- Aphids—These insects are among the most frequently-occurring pests. They feed by tapping into the juice streams in leaves, buds, flowers and even roots, and drawing nutrients away from the plant. Almost any plant is susceptible to aphids.

- Roundworms, nematodes or eelworms— These 1 millimetre-long worms can make their way into flowerpots and plant containers via the potting soil, the plant's soil ball, water, equipment or packaging.

- Scale insects—Their brown shells make scale insects easy to identify; they sit on the undersides of the leaves.
- Mealybugs—These sucking insects, which grow up to 3 mm ($^1/_8$ in) long, produce whitish, wool-like wax secretions which form sticky threads when touched. They use these threads to protect themselves, and lay their eggs inside them. Mealybugs suck out a plant's juices, causing it to gradually become sickly.
- Spider mites—These minute members of the spider family bore into the leaf tissue and feed on the juices they suck out. A typical sign of spider mites is the whitish-grey gossamer in which they sit, and which gradually covers the entire plant. The affected leaves become pale and dry out.
- Thrips—These black and white insects are approximately 2 mm (less than $^1/_8$ in) long. They can be identified by the shiny, silvery discolouration that they leave behind on the plant's leaves.
- White flies—You can see these pests fly out when you touch the plant's leaves.
- Root mealybugs—Indoor gardeners fear these root parasites, since they do their destructive work out of sight. The damage—which in the worst cases can lead to the death of the plant—is usually recognised too late.

Several different types of mites or insects can even attack a plant at the same time.

PROPAGATING YOUR PLANTS

Not only thrifty indoor gardeners will attempt to cultivate new plants themselves rather than buying them. Propagating their favourite plants has always presented a special challenge for amateur gardeners, and provides the grower with a nice feeling of accomplishment when it is successful. You can propagate plants using seeds (generative propagation) or sections of the plant—usually cuttings (vegetative propagation).

A propagating case such as the one above, with a protective glass cover, provides ideal conditions for the tiny, sensitive young plants.

Many houseplants are easy to propagate generatively—that is, via seeds. In the case of generative propagation, you can never be certain that the offspring will be identical to the parent plant.

To perform this type of propagation under home gardening conditions, you will need pots or dishes (preferably 5–7 cm/2–3 in high) with drainage holes. Along with a bright location, you will need a pane of glass to cover the seedlings and an appropriate soil for propagation (rooting substrate). Special miniature greenhouses are also available for the windowsill, some with built-in heaters.

Fill the seedling containers with moist rooting substrate up to 2 cm (³/₄ in) below the rim. Smooth out the surface of the soil and press it down somewhat before sowing the seeds. If the seeds are extremely fine, the top layer of substrate should be sifted. Sprinkle fine seeds loosely; larger seeds should be pressed into the soil individually in rows. Press the surface of the soil down lightly to help the seeds become

integrated into it. In the case of light-sprouting plants (such as African violets, impatiens or cacti) or particularly fine seeds (like begonia seeds) you should cover them only lightly with earth, or not at all. For large seeds, or those that germinate best in darkness (e.g. cyclamen), sift a layer of earth approximately twice as deep as the seeds' diameter over the seeds. Water the planted seeds with a fine spray.

Cover the seed container with a pane of glass or plastic foil to keep the seeds from drying out. You can keep condensed water from dropping down on the seeds by turning the glass or foil over daily. If you have a miniature greenhouse, as mentioned above, this step is not necessary. It is helpful to keep the seed containers in semi-shade until the seeds germinate. The ideal or recommended temperature for germination varies from one plant to another; it ranges between 18 and 22 °C (64–72 °F), and can even be higher in the case of some exotic plants. Germination times are even more variable. Depending on the species, seeds may germinate after ten days, after twenty days, or even after one month; some palm trees require one year to germinate.

When the seedlings develop their first tiny leaves, it is time to transplant them. Use a dibber to carefully lift the individual plantlets out of the soil and replant them in pots, bowls or small boxes. When the plants in the transplant containers grow so large that they begin to touch one another, you can replant them in their more permanent pots or containers.

Pick out the individual seedlings with a dibber and replant them in peat pots before moving them to their final container (left).

The seedlings grow together densely in the sowing tray. You can cultivate a smaller or larger number of seedlings according to your needs with the same effort (below).

Vegetative propagation is actually the most common and logical method for the amateur gardener. With this approach, you do not need to cultivate large numbers of new plants, and you can usually produce strong and healthy offspring from your favourite plants quite quickly and without any problems.

Narcissus (above) are among the most common bulb plants. The bulbs can flourish equally well in pots or in flower beds.

Offshoots (right) develop roots while still attached to the parent plant. They can simply be broken off and planted in pots.

There are a variety of methods for cultivating new plants from parts of another plant:

Division—This method, the simplest form of vegetative propagation, can be employed in any case where the plant expands itself sideways, either by developing new shoots from the root stalk or by sending out rhizomes which continue to grow underground. The best time to divide a plant is at the start of a new growing period—in other words, in spring, when you are likely to be re-potting your plants anyway. Remove the plant you want to divide from its pot and pull the sections apart carefully with your hands, or cut it into sections with a sharp knife. Each section must have sufficient roots and at least one bud. Examples of plants that can be divided without difficulty are asparagus fern and cyperus; mind-your-own-business, sansevieria, cast iron plants and some types of ferns can also be propagated this way.

Propagation via offshoots—Offshoots are stem-like outgrowths that develop on the side of a parent plant (for example, the offsets that develop in members of the pineapple family). They form roots while still attached to the parent plant and continue to grow without any difficulty once they have been separated.

Propagation via plantlets—This method may be even easier than division. Some varieties of plants develop independent plantlets on their leaves, on the edges of leaves or on the leaf stalks; tiny plantlets may even form on flower axes. Once these baby plants have reached a certain stage of development, they fall off and begin living on their own. This type of "live birth" propagation (vivipary) is typical of the piggy-back plant, some types of ferns, kalanchoes and begonias.

Propagation via bulblets—Hyacinths, lilies, narcissus and other bulb plants develop "bulblets" or offsets around the parent bulb; these may be separated and planted in pots.

Propagation via runners—This type of propagation is also simple. Gardeners are familiar with it from strawberry plants, in particular. Some varieties of plants develop offspring on their stem axes, above and below ground—in some cases with very long sections of stem in between the nodes. This phenomenon is typically seen in such plants as the popular spider plant, the saxifrage family and Boston ferns. As soon as the new plantlets are large enough and have sufficient roots, you can separate them and re-pot them in cultivation soil.

Division is a quick and uncomplicated way to propagate your plants. Divide the plant at the level of the root ball, using either your hands or a sharp knife.

Propagation via "mossing"—This somewhat laborious method of propagation can be used for plants with woody stems or for older plants (e.g. a large rubber tree). Make a wedge-shaped cut in the stem or shoot of the parent plant below a leaf node, at the point where you wish to stimulate root growth. The cut should go no deeper than halfway through the stem. Insert a piece of wood into the "wound" to keep it from closing. Then slide over the shoot a plastic bag that is open at both ends (if the steam is very thick you can wrap plastic foil around it). Fasten the bag tightly below the cut, fill it with moist substrate, moss or peat, and then fasten the top as well. As soon as roots have begun to develop—usually within two to three weeks— you can cut off the section of stem or shoot and plant it in a pot. It is best to continue protecting the young plant with plastic foil during the cultivation phase.

Propagation via cuttings—In cutting propagation—in contrast to all the methods described above—root development only takes place after the cuttings are separated from the parent plant. It is the method most frequently used by amateur gardeners, even though it requires some special equipment as well as care. Your chances of success with this type of propagation are greatest in the spring and summer— that is, during the growing phase.

The best soil temperature for rooting cuttings is between 20 and 24 °C (68–75 °F).

Top cuttings: This is the quickest method for obtaining attractive plant offspring. Select mature, non-flowering, green or woody tips of shoots, 5 to 10 cm (2–4 in) long and separate them from the parent plant below just a leaf node, using a sharp knife. For the sake of assimilation, each top cutting should have two to four well-developed leaves.

Section cuttings: In this approach, which is commonly used for hanging or climbing plants, a cutting is taken from the centre or lower section of a shoot. Choose a section of stem

Before cuttings can be taken, a plant needs to have reached a certain level of maturity, with well-developed leaves.

which contains one or more leaves along with the leaf petiole and axil, again cutting it just below a leaf bud. The roots of the new plant will develop out of the axil. Section cuttings take somewhat longer to develop roots than top cuttings do, but they usually result in hardier young plants.

Stem or cane cuttings: This type of propagation employs leafless sections of stem, each of which needs to have at least one dormant axil and one node (the point at which a new leaf stem grows). Lay the 5 to 10 cm (2–4 in) long sections of stem horizontally in a substrate with the axils facing upward and cover them halfway. The roots of the new plant will develop out of the nodes while new shoots develop from the axils. This method works well with such plants as dieffenbachia, dracaena, split-leaf and other types of philodendrons and umbrella trees.

Leaf cuttings: In the case of such plants as foliage begonias, snake plants, kalanchoes and African violets, you can produce new plants by taking cuttings of leaves or sections of leaves. The leaf cuttings form roots and even produce shoots. Cut off a leaf with a fairly short piece of stem and set it vertically or diagonally in cultivation soil.

Propagating cuttings in water: This is another frequently used method which works well with such plants as weeping figs, coleus, spider plants, impatiens or oleander. The transfer of the rooted cuttings from water to soil can constitute a somewhat critical phase, but the plants usually adjust to the change quickly.

Cuttings need to be watered generously in order to promote rapid root development.

To propagate using leaf cuttings, insert the cut edge of the separated leaf into the substrate.

PLANT
COMPENDIUM

ABUTILON
Flowering maple, Velvetleaf, Indian mallow

These abundantly blooming members of the mallow family come from tropical and subtropical regions of Central and South America and have velvety, green or yellow-spotted leaves. The attractive, overhanging, usually bell-form flowers are red, orange, yellow or bi-coloured or may have contrasting darker veins.

In summer the flowering maple enjoys a bright to semi-shady location—outdoors if possible. In winter it likes bright, cool conditions and temperatures around 12 °C (54 °F). Water generously and fertilise twice weekly from spring until autumn; in winter keep the soil just moist. Prune and re-pot in spring. Propagation via cuttings; hybrids via seed.

Species and Types

Abutilon hybrids: green, hand-shaped segmented leaves; e.g. 'Firebell' with red blossoms, 'Golden Fleece' with deep yellow. *A. megapotamicum:* graceful, overhanging branches; attractive hanging plant; yellow and red lantern-form blossoms; 'Aureum' has mottled yellow leaves. *A. striatum:* 'Thompsonii' has salmon coloured, red-veined blossoms, mottled yellow leaves.

> The flowering maple is sensitive to sudden changes in temperature; it reacts by losing its leaves and blossoms. On the other hand, it is prone to mealy bugs, scale insects and spider mites if placed in an over warm location.

ACALYPHA HISPIDA
Chenille plant, Red-hot cattail, Foxtail

All parts of this striking tropical member of the spurge family are poisonous. The chenille plant, with its long, fuzzy clusters of blossoms, prefers a warm and bright location, but is not happy in direct sunlight. Since it requires high humidity, the plant flourishes beautifully in an enclosed plant window. Keep the soil uniformly moist during the growth and flowering periods, but avoid standing water. Fertilise lightly once per week and mist frequently with warm water.

Prune the plant in spring, and re-pot if necessary.

Young shoots that are removed in pruning can be used as cuttings: just plant them in a heated propagating case.

Types

Acalypha hispida 'Alba' has creamy white blossoms. *A. wilkesiana* hybrids, 'Copper-leaf' or 'Jacob's Coat': colourful, decorative foliage plants, e.g. 'Musaica', whose leaves bear a mosaic-like pattern of bronze red and orange-brown.

ACHIMENES
Hot water plant, Widow's tears, Magic flower

The distinctive hot water plant—a member of the gesneriad family—has its origins in the tropics of Central and South America. As its botanical name indicates, it does not tolerate cold temperatures; rather, it is a hothouse plant. Its blossoms sit diagonally on the flower stem and come in a variety of colours and shades from blue to red to white—even yellow varieties exist.

The individual flowers do not last long, but new buds are continually produced, so the plant blooms luxuriously all summer long. This popular pot plant can also be cultivated in a hanging basket.

From spring until autumn, the plant's location should be warm and bright, but it should never receive full sun.

Keep slightly moist with pleasantly warm, preferably soft water; water from below when the plant is in bloom; fertilise approximately every ten days during the growth and flowering period. Beginning in September, the plant will retract its flowers and leaves; you can let it dry out over the winter. Replant the scaly rhizomes in fresh soil in the early spring. A warm substrate is necessary to allow roots to develop.

Propagate by separating the rhizomes or by taking cuttings.

Types

Available types are primarily hybrids, including 'Little Beauty' with small flowers; 'Ambroise Verschaffelt': white with violet veins; 'Rose'.

ADENIUM OBESUM
Desert rose

This member of the dogbane family, from the dry regions of tropical Africa, was named after the city of Aden. The desert rose is actually a succulent, but is often grafted to the related, very similar oleander to increase its growth and abundance of blossoms. You can recognise such plants by the different thicknesses of the two sections. This bizarre plant blossoms in every colour, from pinkish-white to violet to deep purple. There are also bi-coloured varieties. Since its milky sap is highly poisonous, it is best to wear gloves when pruning. Unlike most plants, the desert rose loves full sunlight. You can keep it warm all year long—outdoors in summer as long as it's protected from wind—and somewhat cooler (12–15 °C/54–59 °F) in winter.

Make sure the plant is kept regularly moist; water it only sparingly when placed in a cool location for the winter. Feed with cactus fertiliser every two weeks in the summer. Re-pot only if necessary in the spring. Grafted plants require soil that is rich in nutrients; succulents with their own roots prefer a mixture that contains sand.

ADIANTUM
Maidenhair fern

The maidenhair fern's native habitats are located primarily in tropical and subtropical regions. Its scientific name means that water does not cling to it. The delicate, finely structured leaf fronds branch out from thin, shiny, blackish-brown stems. This very tender plant is just as sensitive as it looks; It grows best in an enclosed plant window or in a small fern garden.

The maidenhair fern requires warmth, shade and high humidity; it will not tolerate any type of draft. Keep it constantly moist with soft, room-temperature water—do not allow the root ball to dry out—but avoid any standing water. The plant should be kept warm over the winter. Supplement with a diluted liquid fertiliser every two weeks from March to August; cut off dried fronds close to the ground. Re-pot in spring. Propagate by dividing the root ball or via spores.

Species and Types

Adiantum raddianum: some interesting cultivars include 'Decorum', the delicately scented 'Fragrantissimum'; 'Goldelse' with green to golden fronds; 'Fritz Lüthi'. *A. tenerum*: fronds are even finer and more delicate, slender form.

AECHMEA FASCIATA
Silver vase bromeliad, Urn plant

This bromeliad is a native of the Brazilian tropics. Its long, slender leaves grow in a rosette formation, creating funnels which collect rainwater. The leaves grow up to 60 cm (24 in) long; they are usually studded with thorns and have silver-grey horizontal stripes. An elegant inflorescence grows in the centre of the funnel, bearing violet-blue blossoms between pink, sheath-like leaves. The plant's weak roots are more an anchor than a means of gaining nutrients.

The urn plant requires a bright location, but without direct sunlight; it prefers room temperature throughout the year. Water and mist with lukewarm, soft water; fertilise every one or two weeks from April to October and change the water in the funnel. In the winter, keep the plant drier and do not fertilise.

It can be propagated by means of offshoots which grow at the base of the parent plant during the blooming period: when the offshoots are half as large as the parent, separate them and their roots and plant them in bromeliad soil; begin watering in their own funnels two weeks before separating.

Species and Types

Aechmea fasciata 'Friederike': thorn-free leaves. *A. chantinii*: one of the most beautiful varieties. *A. fulgens*: coral-coloured blossoms; 'Discolour': the tops of the leaves are olive green and the undersides are violet-red.

AESCHYNANTHUS SPECIOSUS
Lipstick plant, Basket vine

The lipstick plant, a member of the gesneriad family, is an epiphyte (grows on a host plant or tree) in the humid forests from the Himalayas to Indonesia. It's named for its flamboyant blossoms, which are orange-red or even scarlet at their base. The conspicuous, tube-shaped flowers grow in clusters of six to twelve, each of which has four protruding stamens. The lipstick plant is particularly suitable as a hanging plant in a display case or in a climatically controlled plant window.

Consistently warm and semi-shady location (brighter in winter) with high humidity; the plant should not be rotated or moved to another location. Mist frequently with pleasantly warm, soft water; water regularly in summer, less in winter. Supplement with a weak, lime-free fertiliser from March to September; re-pot in spring.

Propagation best via cuttings, which will form roots at soil temperatures of at least 25 °C (77 °F).

Other Species

Aeschynantuhus radicans (= *A. pulcher*) with scarlet flowers; *A. hildebrandii*; *A. tricolor* and a variety of hybrids.

AGERATUM HOUSTONIANUM
Ageratum, Floss flower

Any creature at home in Central America, like the ageratum, requires more light than other species. The plant will accept bright shady conditions at the very least, but it is happiest in direct sunlight. Frost means certain death for this plant, so don't put it in a window box or on the patio until above-freezing temperatures are guaranteed, around mid-May. This abundantly flowering plant is most beautiful in gorgeous shades of blue, but pink and white varieties are also available. Ageratum normally grows up to 30 cm (12 in) and is a popular and long-lasting cut flower. Smaller varieties—with an average height of 15 cm (6 in) —are better suited to window boxes and patios.

The ageratum is not only an industrious grower—it also demands constant attention from the container gardener. If not watered regularly, it will react immediately with stunted growth and a lack of flowers. Fertilise every two weeks, beginning two months after re-potting, at the latest. Propagation via seeds.

Types

'Royal Blue' with dark blue flowers and reddish buds; 'Dondo White'; 'North Sea' with dark purple flowers; 'Blue Heaven'.

An ageratum's willingness to bloom is dependent on a sunny location. Direct sunlight also minimises the risk of botrytis blight.

AGLAONEMA

Chinese evergreen, Spotted evergreen

An attractive member of the arum lily family which is native to the moist and shady tropical forests of East Asia, the Chinese evergreen is frequently confused with its close relative, the dieffenbachia. Its large, evergreen leaves are usually ornately patterned and mottled. The blossoms consist of an arum-like flower spadix enclosed by a spathe, and are relatively modest in appearance. In some varieties, pretty, gleaming-red poisonous berries form if the plant is pollinated. The Chinese evergreen contains substances irritating to the skin and mucous membranes.

The Chinese evergreen also grows extremely well in hydroponic culture. The ideal location for this plant is an enclosed plant window or a hothouse with a lot of indirect humidity. It requires a shady to semi-shady location, at or above room temperature; the air and soil temperature should not fall below 16 to 18 °C (61–64 °F). Keep consistently moist with soft, room-temperature water; water less in the winter. Fertilise sparingly from spring until August; in spring, re-pot in wide, shallow containers as necessary.

Species and Types

Aglaonema commutatum: native to Java and the Philippines, silver-green striped, mottled or speckled, stems 50 cm (20 in) high; 'Silver King', 'Silver Queen', 'San Remo', 'Pseudobracteatum'. *A. costatum*: a native of Malaysia, its stems are bushy and branched at the base.

> The Chinese evergreen's susceptibility to pests can usually be traced back to mistakes made in its care, allowing mealybugs, scale insects or spider mites to take over.

ALLAMANDA CATHARTICA

Golden trumpet, Allamanda

The golden trumpet, with its shiny yellow, fragrant, funnel-shaped flowers, is a tropical dogbane native to the Brazilian rainforests. All parts of the plant are poisonous. The golden trumpet is a very fast-growing creeping shrub. It develops sturdy shoots several metres long and requires a climbing support.

This plant flourishes best in a hothouse or winter garden: it requires very bright light, high humidity and warmth; it will tolerate slightly cooler temperatures in winter, but must be protected from drafts. Water and mist regularly with lukewarm water from April to September and fertilise sparingly once a week. During the winter rest period, keep the plant somewhat drier; re-pot in spring.

Propagate via top cuttings in the spring or autumn.

Types

'Hendersonii': deep orange-yellow; 'Grandiflora': lemon yellow; 'Schottii': extremely fast-growing.

ALOE
Aloe

It's hard to believe, but these thorny-looking plants are actually members of the lily family: aloe grows on the steppes of South Africa, Madagascar and Arabia. Their shape is similar to the agave, but their fleshy leaves—which grow in a rosette formation, overlapping like roof shingles—live on after the plant has flowered and produced seeds. Older plants blossom regularly: the flowers are tube or bell-shaped and grow in grape-like clusters on a high stalk. The plant's bitter juice relieves pain and cramps and is a traditional remedy for wounds, particularly burns.

The aloe plant loves full sun and enjoys a warm outdoor location sheltered from rain in summer. In winter it prefers cool temperatures—from 6 to 10 °C (43–50 °F)—and it tolerates dry air well.

Water moderately from spring through autumn; keep it nearly dry in winter. Avoid standing water, and do not water the leaves. Add a little cactus fertiliser to the water every two to three weeks in the summer; re-pot in the spring if necessary.

Propagate by taking shoots from the side of the plant, or via seeds.

Species

Aloe variegata, tiger or partridge breast aloe: from South Africa, up to 30 cm (12 in) high, triangular, dark green leaves with white-spotted ribbon pattern, red flowers. *A. arborescens,* candelabra aloe or tree aloe: well-known healing plant, forms stems and many branches, up to 50 cm (20 in) high, leaves have thorny edges. *A. barbadensis,* aloe vera or burn plant: juice is beneficial to the skin.

ANANAS
Pineapple

Pineapple has its origins in the tropical regions of Central and South America, where it is an important food. There, its rosettes grow to 2 metres (7 ft) in diameter. The ornamental plants raised for indoor gardens are smaller; but with their sharp, thorny-edged leaves, they still require a great deal of space. A flower axis grows out of the middle of the leaf rosette only in older plants. This develops into a multiple fruit topped with a crown of leaves; the fruits have a fragrant aroma. Once the fruit has matured, the plant sends out offshoots and the parent plant dies shortly afterwards.

Pineapple prefers to stand in a bright location (but without direct noonday sun in the summer) and room temperature all through the year. Water generously in summer with soft, room-temperature water, but water sparingly in winter. In summer, fertilise only moderately every two weeks; re-pot them every two years.

It propagates via offshoots, which must be half as large as the parent plant. Alternatively, you can root the leafy top of the fruit in sandy soil with a ground temperature of 25 °C (77 °F); the cut surface should be allowed to dry before planting.

Species and Types

Ananas comosus, 'Aureo-Variegatus': green, yellow and white vertical stripes tinged with pink; does not grow very large. *A. bracteatus:* smaller, with a thick red tuft of leaves on the fruit; 'Striatus': green and yellow striped. *A. nanus:* 20 to 30 cm (8–12 in) high.

ANTHURIUM
Anthurium, Tail flower, Flamingo flower

Anthurium scherzianum, an elegant member of the arum lily family, is native to the tropical American rainforests. Its name comes from the Greek *anthos* (flower), and *oura* (tail). What appears to be a flower petal is, in fact, a spathe—usually red in colour. The actual flowers are very small and are clustered together on a spadix, which is twisted into a spiral form—giving this plant the nickname, 'pigtail anthurium'. The heart or lancet-shaped leaves are a shiny dark green, creating an attractive contrast to the striking spathe. Anthuriums bloom all year long, but a short, cooler rest period is advisable in winter. The plant grows slowly and is well suited to windowsills, dormer windows and plant windows.

The anthurium's location should be bright to semi-shady, but without direct sun; it likes a constant temperature of 15 to 18 °C (59–64 °F). Keep the soil moist during the growing phase, but avoid standing water; do not use cold or hard water. Mist the leaves but not the flowers. This plant is well-suited to hydroponic culture. Fertilise lightly once a week in the summer. When the roots become pot-bound, re-pot in spring in a special anthurium substrate.

Propagation: divide when re-potting; cuttings from separate offshoots which have formed roots; seed propagation is also possible.

Other Species and Hybrids

Of *Anthurium Scherzerianum* hybrids, the little flamingo flower, is the best-known. *A. andreanum*, the large flamingo flower, is larger with shiny spathes ranging from red to white; older plants form aerial roots. *A. crystallinum*: a foliage plant nicely suited to plant windows with large, heart-shaped, white-veined leaves.

APHELANDRA SQUARROSA
Zebra plant

This tropical member of the acanthus family comes from Brazil. Its brilliant yellow flower heads protrude from the bracts, which grow in an overlapping, roof-shingle formation. Shiny dark green leaves with white veins form an attractive contrast.

The zebra plant loves bright, but not sunny conditions; it should be kept moist and warm except for an eight-week rest period in winter when conditions should be cooler. The plant flourishes well in a greenhouse.

During the growth period, water often and well with soft, room-temperature water; water less in winter. Wash the leaves periodically and mist them daily. Fertilise weekly during the growth period. Prune and re-pot in March.

Propagate via top and axil cuttings planted in a warm propagating case.

Other Species and Types

'Leopoldii' has reddish stalks; 'Fritz Prinsler': an interesting new variety; *A. sinclairiana* and *A. tetragona* bloom red in your plant window.

APOROCACTUS FLAGELLIFORMIS
Rat's tail cactus

This decorative cactus owes its name to its shoots, which can reach 1.5 metres (5 ft) in length. In its native Mexico, it grows in mountainous regions at altitudes up to 2500 metres (8000 ft). The green shoots studded with tiny thorns bear blossoms ca. 10 cm (4 in) long, ranging from pink to red.

The rat's tail cactus is ideal for a hanging pot. Hang it in a bright, sunny location, but not directly in the midday sun. In summer it prefers to be outdoors; in winter, it requires a rest period in a bright location at temperatures of 10 to 15 °C (50–59 °F). Water generously in summer and supplement with cactus fertiliser every two weeks. The plant should be kept nearly dry in winter, but in humid air. Don't rotate the plant when it is forming buds or blossoming; re-pot as infrequently as possible.

As one might expect from a cactus, the rat's tail cactus enjoys a warm location. However, if the air becomes too dry, it can quickly become infested with spider mites. Therefore, always ensure that the humidity is high.

ARAUCARIA HETEROPHYLLA
Norfolk Island pine

The Norfolk Island pine, of the araucaria family, was discovered by Captain Cook in 1775 on an island in the South Pacific, where it grows up to 60 metres (200 ft) high. This conifer has layers of horizontally growing branches.

The Norfolk Island pine needs a semi-shady—not sunny— location with high humidity. It needs to stand freely or it will grow only on one side. It does not tolerate pruning well. Keep it fairly warm in summer, even when outdoors; gradually transfer to a cooler winter location with temperatures of 5 to 10 °C (41–50 °F). Keep it moist from spring to autumn, using softened water. Water sparingly in winter; mist frequently. Fertilise lightly in March through August; re-pot only every two to three years, or less for older plants.

ARDISIA CRENATA
Coral ardisia, Coralberry, Spice berry, Hen's eyes

This charming miniature evergreen tree, a member of the myrsine family, has its origins in the shady forests of tropical Southeast Asia. Its most attractive feature is its shiny, red, pea-shaped berries, which it often retains till the following summer. The short-lived, red and white umbels are fairly unprepossessing.

The coral ardisia requires a bright location without full sunlight; moderately warm, but somewhat cooler in the winter.

Keep moist with lukewarm water in the summer; moderately moist in winter. Ensure humid air by misting it regularly (but not during the blossoming period). Fertilise sparingly every two weeks during the vegetative period; re-pot in the spring.

Propagation via seeds or cuttings.

> You can counteract the coral ardisia's susceptibility to scale insects and mealybugs by washing its leaves and branches with soapy water.

ASPARAGUS
Asparagus fern

Like its close relative, the garden asparagus, *Asparagus densiflorus* 'Sprengeri' belongs to the lily family. Its pale green, needle-shaped foliage does not actually consist of leaves, but of tiny stems called cladophylls. Its thick roots are capable of storing water. When well tended the asparagus fern develops small red, poisonous berries in the autumn. Its name comes from the Greek *asparagos* (asparagus) and *densiflorus* (thick-blooded). The plant originally comes from Southeast Africa. Since it is very long-lasting and grows rapidly, gardeners often use asparagus fern for cut foliage. In the home, it looks particularly attractive in a hanging basket.

The asparagus fern flourishes best in a semi-shady to bright location, but without full sun. It enjoys fresh air in the summer: You can place the plant outdoors as long as it is protected from direct sunlight.

The little "leaves" lose moisture quickly and require a great deal of water, so you should water the plant generously, especially in the summer; do not allow the root ball to dry out. Fertilise the plant once per week, less in the winter. Re-pot the asparagus fern every year in the spring—less frequently for older plants.

Propagate via division or with seeds, ideally in April.

Species and Types

Asparagus densiflorus 'Meyeri' has foxtail-shaped shoots. In *A. densiflorus* 'Myriocladus', the "needles" grow in thick bunches. *A. setaceus* (*A. plumosus*), or 'Plumosa asparagus fern', is a variety with delicate, highly decorative "tails". *A. falcatus* is a climbing variety; it is very sturdy and bears sickle-shaped cladophylls that can grow up to 10 cm (4 in) long.

ASPIDISTRA ELATIOR
Cast iron plant, Bar room plant

One of our oldest houseplants is the familiar cast iron plant, a member of the lily family that is native to the forests of East Asia. Its evergreen, sword-shaped leaves—which can grow up to 50 cm (20 in) long—grow individually on tall stalks; the brownish-violet blossoms lie inconspicuously on the ground.

The names 'cast iron plant' or 'bar room plant' refer to the fact that this highly tolerant plant is so nearly indestructible that it could traditionally tolerate even the dimly-lit conditions of a bar room.

In fact, the cast iron plant can flourish practically anywhere: it requires very little light and can even tolerate drafts or very dry air. Its ideal location is cool, but it can also survive in a warm environment. Dust the leaves regularly; keep only moderately moist; fertilise lightly every two weeks in the spring and summer; re-pot every two or three years.

Propagate in the spring by dividing carefully.

The 'Variegata' variety, with white to yellow-white striped leaves, requires more light than the standard variety.

ASPLENIUM NIDUS
Bird's nest fern

The decorative bird's nest fern grows epiphytically in the treetops of tropical rainforests. Its name refers to the nest-shaped centre of its rosette of leaves, where (like the bromeliads) it collects rainwater and nutrients. Its shiny, light green, non-segmented fronds have a dark central rib at their base; they stand upright and can grow to heights of over a metre (3 ft) in the plant's natural habitat.

The ideal location for this plant is an enclosed plant window, where you can place it on a heated surface or an epiphyte stalk. The bird's nest fern requires warm conditions, partial shade and above all, high humidity.

Water with lukewarm, softened water—generously in the summer, less so in winter. Fertilise lightly every two weeks; re-pot every two years in the summer. Do not use any shiny foliage sprays!

Propagates via spores.

Other Species and Types

'Fimbriatur' also tolerates dry air. The following varieties develop young plants on their pinnate fronds, which grow roots and may be re-potted: *Asplenium bulbiferum*, *A. daucifolium* (Mother fern), *A. dimorphum*. The latter variety is particularly hardy.

ASTROPHYTUM

Star cactus, Sea urchin cactus, Bishop's cap

These popular, undemanding Mexican cacti take a variety of shapes—from flat ball to cylinder—may be ribbed and often bear white tufts of hair.

Their scientific name means "star plant". The summer flowers are yellow.

Place the hairy or thorny varieties in a bright spot, pro-

tected from direct sunlight; the green, thornless varieties prefer semi-shade. All types like warm conditions in summer and bright and cool conditions in winter, at temperatures of 8 to 10 °C (46–50 °F). Water with softened water in summer, keep dry in winter; the plant prefers dry air. If necessary, re-pot young plants in the winter in a substrate containing more minerals than humus.

Propagates via seeds.

Species

Astrophytum myriostigma or bishop's cap: segmented with five ribs, has no thorns, but

bears plushy tufts of hair distributed over the whole plant; reaches heights up to 15 cm (6 in), light yellow flowers. *A. asterias* or sea urchin cactus: flat ball shape with eight very flat ribs, each bearing a row of white, woolly tufts; no thorns, grows slowly, 4 cm (1½ in) tall, yellow flowers. *A. ornatum*: long shape, conspicuously ribbed; hard, sharp thorns, shiny yellow flowers. *A. capricorne*, goat's horn cactus: covered with white, woolly tufts; long, tangled thorns; bright yellow flowers with a deep red calyx.

BEGONIA

Begonia

Most of the more than 1,000 members of the begonia family originated in the tropics. We make a distinction between foliage begonias and flowering begonias. Place the plants in a bright location, but not in direct sunlight. They require a great deal of indirect humidity but do not mist the leaves. Do not rotate; the plants will not tolerate smoke or drafts. Keep them uniformly moist; fertilise lightly every two weeks from March through September. Re-pot in spring; prune back leggy varieties before re-potting.

Begonias are propagated primarily via leaf cuttings; how-

ever, top cuttings or rhizome division are also possible.

Species and Types

Foliage begonias

Rex hybrids (Rex begonias): classical foliage begonias with abundant, colourful leaves; re-

warding houseplants. 'Bettina Rothschild' has reddish purple edges; 'Comtesse Louise Erdody' has leaves that spiral inward at the base. *Boweri* hybrids: 'Cleopatra', with beautiful multi-coloured leaves;

'Tiger', reddish-brown with greenish-yellow spots; 'Nigramarga'. *Mexicross* hybrids are crossings with South American varieties.

Begonia imperialis: low-growing, very fuzzy leaves

with a velvety shine; *B. heracleifolia* with deeply grooved leaves; *B. foliosa* has many small, shiny leaves.

Flowering begonias

Elatior hybrids: the most popular group, they can be purchased in bloom all year long; usually cultivated only as annuals. 'Alma': fiery orange; 'Renaissance': red. *Rieger* begonias are the most modern variety and less sensitive than others: 'Schwabenland': red; 'Aphrodite': red and pink, a hanging plant; 'Goldstar': yellow. *Lorraine* hybrids: 'Gloire de Lorraine' bears small pink blossoms in winter. *Corallina* hybrids: The trout begonia has white spotted leaves and bright pink or red flowers, leggy growth; two are 'Luzerna' or 'Madame Charrat'.

BELLIS PERENNIS CULTIVARS
English daisy

These pretty perennial relatives of the lawn daisy display their single or compound blossoms in shades of pink or white from spring—usually in March—until summer. The size of the flowers is as variable as their colour. Their fresh, delicate appearance makes them ideal companions for primroses, pansies or forget-me-nots. They are not fussy about location: they tolerate full sunlight just as well as semi-shade. However, the seeds definitely require light in order to germinate.

Avoid excessive watering; it is better to keep them barely moist, especially while there is a risk of frost. If you re-pot the plants in new substrate every year, you will scarcely need to fertilise them.

Propagates via seeds in the summer.

Types

'White Pomponette', 'Pink Pomponette' and 'Red Pomponette'.

> Although English daisies are otherwise unproblematic, aphids or fungi may attack their long white stems. This is most likely to occur when the plant's location is too warm.

BELOPERONE GUTTATA
Shrimp plant, False hop, Brandgee

This member of the acanthus family, a native of the Mexican tropics, is a pretty and rewarding houseplant. Its overlapping yellow, brown and red spathes—which resemble hops flowers—are particularly distinctive. The white true flowers emerge from between the spathes, but fall off rather quickly. This plant likes very bright conditions, but not direct sunlight. A warm location—preferably a patio—is best in summer; it should be kept cooler in winter. Water generously in the spring and summer, and fertilise weekly. In autumn and winter, withhold fertiliser and water more sparingly. Prune in spring; repot as necessary.

Propagate using pruned cuttings, which will form roots in warm soil; seed propagation is also possible.

BILLBERGIA NUTANS
Queen's tears, Friendship plant

One of the most undemanding members of the pineapple family is the decorative queen's tears. It originates in tropical rainforests from Mexico to Brazil, where—atypically for bromeliads—it grows on the surface of the soil. Also unlike most bromeliads, its flower axes bow down toward the ground. The inconspicuous green-violet flowers, whose long filaments extend from their centres, are surrounded by showy, deep pink spathes. The plant's flowering period depends on the temperature during the winter. Its leaves are small, sometimes grass-like and hanging, making queen's tears suitable for hanging baskets as well.

This hardy plant prefers a bright location at room temperature throughout the year (this is especially true of the hybrid varieties); however, it can also spend the summer in a well-sheltered location outdoors. It even tolerates dry air! Water generously with lukewarm water in the summer (the funnel should always contain fresh water); water less in winter if the location is cool. Fertilise weekly in the summer and re-pot as necessary in wide, flat containers filled with potting soil. Propagates via offshoots.

BLECHNUM GIBBUM
Tree fern, Palm fern, Blechnum

The tree fern, a native of New Caledonia, has a funnel-shaped rosette of green, feathery fronds and is similar in appearance to a palm tree. The stem emerges from the creeping root stalk and often grows diagonally or horizontally. A mature tree fern can reach a height of several metres.

The tree fern requires a semi-shady spot and high humidity. Location and soil should both be warm—room temperature or above; even in winter, temperatures should not fall below 18 °C (64 °F). Keep the soil consistently moist in summer using room-temperature water. Water slightly less in winter, but don't let the root ball dry out. Fertilise with a very weak concentrate every two weeks from April to August; re-pot in March if needed. Propagates via spores at soil temperatures between 20 °C and 25 °C (68–77 °F); it may also be divided.

Other Species

Blechnum brasiliense requires higher humidity; its young fronds are reddish-brown. *B. moorei.*

BOUGAINVILLEA
Bougainvillea

This gorgeous climbing plant originates in Brazil and is a member of the four-o'clock family. Its strikingly coloured, paper-thin spathes can range from brilliant red-violet to white, salmon-coloured, pink and red. They surround the small, yellow-and-white flowers in groups of three. Bougainvillea can be grown on a round frame or trellis, as a pot plant or as a high-stemmed tree; in the wild, it grows into a tree that is 3 to 4 metres (10–13 ft) high.

A Bougainvillea's location should always be bright and airy: sunny and warm in the summer, in an outdoor loca-

tion that is protected from wind and rain. In winter, the plant requires a rest period at temperatures of 8 to 10 °C (46–50 °F).

Water generously in the summer and fertilise once a week. Prune and re-pot in March. Move the plant only as much as necessary.

Propagation via cuttings is difficult.

Species

Bougainvillea spectabilis: fast-growing, thorny, with red-violet spathes; does not grow well indoors. *B. glabra*: pink spathes; 'Variegata' has coloured leaves; 'Snow White' has white spathes.

BROWALLIA SPECIOSA
Bush violet, Sapphire flower, Amethyst flower, Star flower

The bush violet, a member of the nightshade family, is a pretty half-shrub from the tropics of South America. The white-throated flowers range in colour from blue to blue-violet; there are also white varieties. The bush violet is a poisonous plant. It is usually cultivated as an annual.

Its location should be airy and bright, but it will not tolerate direct midday sun. Remove wilted blossoms immediately; keep the soil moderately moist at all times and fertilise every two weeks.

Propagation takes place via seeds, usually in February. You can regulate the flow-

ering period by adjusting the sowing time. It is best to plant several seedlings in each pot. Propagation via cuttings is also possible.

Other Species

Browallia viscosa and *B. grandiflora* are also suitable for the garden.

If you begin to supporting your bush violet when it is young, it will branch out and reward you with beautiful, luxuriant flowers. Removing wilted flowers and leaves immediately stimulates the plant to produce more blossoms and extends the flowering.

BRUNFELSIA PAUCIFLORA

Yesterday, today & tomorrow; Morning, noon & night

This attractive, slightly fragrant plant is native to the tropical regions of Central and South America, so it prefers high humidity. The magnificent blossoms of this poisonous nightshade plant vary from violet, blue, white and yellow, depending upon the variety. Its dark green, leathery leaves are evergreen; it produces very large seeds.

An ideal location for this plant is a plant window that is bright but not sunny and consistently, moderately warm all year round.

Water regularly with warm, soft water in the summer, and fertilise every week or two. Keep cooler from November to January. Prune back after the blooming period.

Propagate via cuttings in summer.

Types

'Calycina' is the predominant type. 'Macrantha' bears flowers that change from lilac blue to white.

BUXUS SEMPERVIRENS

Common box, Boxwood, Box tree

The boxwood's natural habitat is Central Europe, North Africa and the Caucasus. Until a few years ago, it was used primarily as a border for garden beds or paths; nowadays, it is equally prized as a single plant in a pot on the patio or beside the front door. Boxwood is an evergreen plant. It is relatively hardy—that is, it is completely resistant to frost and is content in any location.

Fertilise once with a slow-release fertiliser in the spring. The only sin this plant will not forgive is standing water in the root area. Therefore, water moderately, but don't let the plant dry out. In order to maintain the boxwood's attractive, compact shape prune it regularly: August is the most practical time. Cut older specimens back to a height of 30 cm (12 in) to allow new shoots to develop.

Propagate in summer, taking semi-mature cuttings that are approximately 10 cm (4 in) high.

Species and Types

Buxus microphylla from Japan, *B. arborescens,* 'Handworthiensis', 'Elegantissima', 'Suffruticosa', 'Glauca', 'Argento variegata', 'Aureo variegata'.

> The boxwood is often threatened by box rust (*Puccinia buxi*), which appears in the autumn in the form of dark brown spots. Remove and destroy any affected leaves.

CALADIUM
Caladium

This South American member of the arum lily family displays richly coloured patterns on its heart- or arrow-shaped, long-stemmed leaves. The flowers, in contrast, are green and inconspicuous. Caladium is especially happy in a hot-house or an enclosed plant window; the location should be bright to semi-shady, but not sunny. The plant requires consistent warmth and very humid air; however, you should not mist the sensitive leaves. Fertilise and water regularly with warm water in summer. The caladium's leaves dry out in the autumn, and the plant requires a rest period. Allow the tubers to dry out and keep the plant at a temperature of at least 18 °C (64 °F) over the winter. Soon after they begin to sprout after the winter, divide the tubers and re-pot them.

Hybrids

Bicolor hybrids have unusually large, brightly coloured leaves with long stems. *Schomburgkii* hybrids have arrow-shaped leaves.

CALATHEA
Calathea

This beautiful member of the prayer plant family comes from the tropical rainforests. Its botanical name comes from the Greek *kalathos* (basket). Its large, silver to dark-green, coloured and patterned leaves are evergreen; flowers may appear in the spring or early summer.

The calathea is most at home in a hothouse or enclosed plant window. The location needs to be semi-shady with high humidity; temperatures should be warm to very warm. It will tolerate a slightly cooler location in winter; avoid drafts.

Water generously, particularly in the summer; fertilise every two weeks during the growing period. Re-pot in a porous humus substrate once a year, ideally in the spring. You can also propagate the plant by division at this time.

Species and Types

Calathea makoyana, peacock plant: one of the most beautiful foliage plants, it has a dark green pattern on a creamy white ground. *C. lancifolia*: lancet-shaped leaves with alternating large and small, dark olive green speckles; the undersides of the leaves are purple. *C. ornate*, 'Roseolineata': dark green with narrow, rose-coloured stripes between its secondary veins; these later turn silvery white. *C. picturata*, 'Argentea': silvery-white leaf surface with green edges. *C. zabrina*: velvety shine, patterned in light and dark green. *C. crocata*: striking orange flowers, green leaves with dark red down.

CALCEOLARIA
Lady's slipper, Slipperwort, Pocketbook plant

This cheerfully blooming member of the figwort family from the cool, moist South American mountains is known for the unusual shape of its flowers. The lower lip of the throat-shaped blossom forms a wide "slipper" shape—hence its botanical name, the Latin *calceolus* (little shoe). The lady's slipper is an eye-catching houseplant in all its variations—whether in one or two colours, speckled or striped, in shades ranging from yellow to deep red. Unfortunately, this plant only lasts for a single season. It is therefore better to buy a plant bearing many buds than one that is in full bloom.

The lady's slipper likes bright conditions without direct sunlight, cool temperatures (12–15 °C/54–59 °F) and plenty of air—but no drafts!

Water evenly (not the leaves); avoid standing water. Pick wilted blossoms; fertilise often.

Species and Types

Calceolaria hybrids: 'Gmündener Melodie' provides a gleaming array of colours; 'Color-Toffel' is a large-flowering variety. *C. integrifolia* is suitable for balconies and gardens; may be propagated via cuttings.

CALENDULA OFFICINALIS
Pot marigold, Calendula

These annual plants are native to Southern Europe Their bright, compound blossoms are found in every shade of yellow and orange. The plant displays itself in all its glory when placed in direct sunlight. A shady location results in fewer flowers, but the plant will tolerate it. When temperatures fall below 5 °C (41 °F), the marigold's flowering days are over. It is a versatile addition to floral arrangements in pots or dishes, since there are types ranging in height from 20 cm to 60 cm (8–24 in).

Water marigolds as soon as the surface of the soil begins to be dry: this may be twice a day on very hot days. Weekly doses of fertiliser encourage the plant to bloom abundantly: begin two months after planting. Like most balcony plants, marigolds will repay you for diligently removing wilted blossoms by blooming all the more luxuriantly. Cutting the entire plant back to about 7 cm (3 in) at the end of the first flowering period, encourages it to bloom again.

Propagation via seeds.

Types

'Orange Gitana' and 'Yellow Gitana': 20 to 30 cm (8–12 in) high; 'Pacific beauty' and 'Princess': 50 to 60 cm (20–24 in) high.

> Mosaic virus manifests itself in the form of round, pale yellow spots which cover the entire plant. Burn any affected marigold plants and clean the pots thoroughly. You will need to change the substrate, since it can carry virus spores.

CALLISTEMON CITRINUS
Lemon bottle brush, Crimson bottle brush

This Australian myrtle takes its unusual name from the shape of its inflorescence: the flower axes resemble the brushes used for cleaning bottles.

The striking scarlet "bristles" are actually multiple stamens. The true blossoms are yellow-green and inconspicuous; they form axes up to 10 cm (4 in) long. If you crush the bottle brush's evergreen, lancet-shaped leaves, they will give off an intense lemony scent. Even young plants will bloom abundantly in the summer. In the summer, the bottle brush enjoys a sunny, airy and warm location outdoors; in winter, it likes a cool room with temperatures between 6 and 10 °C (43–50 °F). Water regularly with softened water, less in the winter. Use a low-lime fertiliser every one or two weeks in the summer. Re-pot if necessary in spring in a humus, low-lime substrate.

Propagate via cuttings in a heated propagating case.

CALLUNA VULGARIS
Heather

This undemanding dwarf shrub is well known as a member of the heather family, which has its origins all over Europe and in the steppes and foothill regions of Asia. Heather can grow up to 80 cm (30 in) high and bears thick clusters of tiny white, pink or red bell-shaped flowers.

The flowering period varies according to the cultivated type and ranges from the end of May through October. The normally winter-hardy heather is well suited to balcony boxes or plant containers and dishes for the patio. It does not do well in interior spaces or winter gardens.

Heather flourishes well in acidic, sandy soil in a sunny to semi-shady location. Fertilise it very sparingly in the spring and keep it slightly moist during the summer. Take care that the root ball does not dry out in winter. Heather needs to be cut back at the end of the flowering period to ensure that it will bloom again.

Propagate via seeds in spring or cuttings in the summer.

CAMELLIA JAPONICA
Camellia

This magnificent member of the tea family, from the cool mountain forests of Japan, reached Europe as early as the 19th century. Today there are more than 10,000 single, double, and compound flower varieties in existence, in every shade from white to dark red. The rose-like, non-fragrant blossoms appear from November through March; the shiny, dark green, leathery foliage is evergreen.

Camellias are delicate: above all, they need consistency in every aspect of their care. They prefer airy, cool, and bright to semi-shady condi-

tions throughout the year with moderate humidity. In summer they do best outdoors. Do not rotate the plant, since its buds will turn toward the sun. Keep it uniformly moist with softened water; fertilise with lime-free fertiliser every two weeks in the growth phase until buds are formed. Re-pot when the roots reach the top of the pot. Keep the plant below 10 °C (50 °F) in winter. Propagate by taking top cuttings containing three leaves.

Types
'Chandleri Elegans': a classic pink variety; 'Alba Simplex': white, single-layered blos-

soms; 'Mathotiana': red, double blossoms; 'Donation': marbled pink; 'Golden Spangles': two-toned leaves. Today, *Williamsii* hybrids are

also available. *Camellia sasanqua*: a slow-growing variety, it develops elegant, overhanging branches and begins blooming in October.

CAMPANULA
Bellflower, Campanula

Everyone recognises the dainty bellflower from the Mediterranean regions: this flow-

er's entire family bears its name, which is derived from the Latin *campanula* ("little

bell"). The delicate, bell-shaped blossoms appear from March to August. The plant's fragile stems contain a sticky, white, non-poisonous, milky sap. Its hanging form makes the campanula a natural for hanging baskets.

Campanulas can tolerate quite hard water and prefer an airy, bright or even sunny location but they must be protected from drafts and direct sun.

The plant may be placed outdoors in the summer; in winter, it requires a cool, frost-free room.

Water campanulas according to the temperature—that is,

generously in the summer and very little in winter. They appreciate fertiliser every one or two weeks in the summer; cut back in the spring and re-pot if necessary.

Propagate using the cuttings taken when pruning, or via division.

Species and Types
Campanula isophylla is a native of the Ligurian Alps and has star-shaped flowers; 'Mayi': blue-violet; 'Alba': white. *C. fragilis*: blue flowers. *C. pyramidalis*, 'Jacob's Ladder': biennial, reaches a height of up to 1.5 m (5 ft). *C. poscharskyana*.

CAPSICUM ANNUM

Ornamental pepper, Cayenne pepper, Paprika

This charming little shrub, a member of the nightshade family, originates in the American tropics, where it can grow up to 2 metres (7 ft) tall. It is a close relative of the bell pepper. Its small, nodding blossoms are white or yellowish, but the plant's true attraction is its decorative fruits, which appear in the autumn. The shiny, leathery little peppers range in colour from creamy white to yellow, orange, red and even violet. Depending on the variety they may be round, cylindrical or pointed, upright or hanging.

The fruit has a very hot, spicy flavour; the green parts of the plant are poisonous.

Ornamental peppers enjoy bright, sunny, airy and moderately warm locations—cool in the winter. They can easily go outdoors in summer.

Keep consistently moist, water lightly once a week during the growing period. There is no need to re-pot since the ornamental pepper—as its botanical name (*annuum*) indicates—is unfortunately an annual.

Propagate in the spring via seeds.

CARYOTA MITIS

Fishtail palm

The fishtail palm, a native of Southeast Asia, is a rarity among the palms. Its feathery leaves resemble fish tails that have been nibbled on. Its growth is slow, bushy and multi-stemmed: it can reach heights of several metres in its natural habitat; in ideal conditions in the home, it can grow up to 1.5 metres (5 ft) tall. In nature, the mature plants develop striking, dark green fruit axes which look like bunches of nuts strung together.

The distinctive fishtail palm requires a warm location (no cooler than 18 °C/64 °F) with high humidity but without direct sunlight throughout the year; an enclosed plant window or a greenhouse is ideal. Always keep the soil evenly moist and ensure that the plant has good drainage. Fertilise lightly in the summer. Re-pot only when the roots become pot-bound.

Propagate via seeds or offshoots.

> Although the fishtail palm lends your home a distinctive look, it is not entirely easy to care for. Like many plants from hot, moist climates, it requires high humidity, which you can provide through frequent misting. Otherwise the plant will be susceptible to spider mite attacks.

CATTLEYA
Cattleya, Cattleya orchid

About 40 varieties of this enchanting member of the orchid family exist in the American tropics, and a huge assortment of hybrids have been cultivated from them; all are gloriously colourful and have a distinctive lower lip. In the wild cattleyas live in trees as epiphytes. With proper care, they

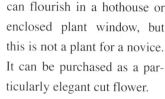

can flourish in a hothouse or enclosed plant window, but this is not a plant for a novice. It can be purchased as a particularly elegant cut flower.

Cattleya's location should be airy and bright, but not in direct sunlight. High humidity is a necessity. The plant requires warmth in the daytime; at night, it should be a few degrees cooler; it should be somewhat warmer in summer than in winter.

Water with soft water in summer; immerse in water regularly. Fertilise lightly once a month; water sparingly in winter. Cattleya should be given a

rest period after it flowers. Repot in orchid soil every two to three years: spring and summer-bloomers after their blooming period, autumn and winter bloomers in the spring.

Propagate via pseudobulbs at the time of re-potting.

Species and Hybrids

Labiata hybrids: autumn-blooming, violet-pink with a cream-coloured lip; 'Candida': white. *Cattleya bowringiana*: autumn-blooming, pink to violet shades, brown stripe on the lip, easy to cultivate. *C. trianaei*: winter-blooming. Multi-species hybrids include *Laeliocattleya*.

CEPHALOCEREUS SENILIS
Old man cactus, Old man of Mexico

The best-known of the tufted cactus family is the original old man cactus of Mexico. In place of thorns it has greyish-white hair that may be 12 cm (5 in) long. Its pink-white, unpleasantly scented blossoms first appear when it reaches 5 to 6 metres (16–20 ft); in the wild it gets up to 15 metres (50 ft) tall. Old man cactus is a plant for experienced cactus gardeners and should be in a greenhouse or plant window. Conditions should be bright all year. Protect the plant from drafts and dirt; it loves limey soil. Keep it very warm and moist in summer and mist

frequently; give it cactus fertiliser biweekly from April to June. Temperatures shouldn't drop below 15 °C (59 °F) in winter; keep the plant nearly dry. Re-pot carefully, once a year for younger plants, less often for older ones.

Propagate via seeds in sandy soil.

> The humidity should not be too low in the summer, or the plant will become infested with spider mites and mealybugs. Conversely, in winter, too much humidity can cause the cactus to rot and mould.

CEREUS
Saguaro cactus, Cereus cactus, Night-blooming cereus

The name "Cereus" means "wax candle" and refers to the white, sea green or blue layer of wax that covers this cactus and protects it from losing its moisture. In addition, some varieties grow, straight as candles, to heights of several metres in their native South American habitat. The saguaro cactus is easy to cultivate and works well as a grafting base. Its magnificent flowers open only at night.

The saguaro cactus requires dry air and sun: in the summer, it should be placed in a warm spot in full sunlight, even outdoors. In the winter, its location should be very cool. Water it moderately in the summer and fertilise occasionally. Water only sparingly or not at all in winter; re-pot the saguaro no more than every few years.

Propagate via seeds or cuttings: allow cut off edges to dry out before planting.

Species and Types

Cereus jamacaru: a native of Brazil, bluish wax layer, white blossoms; dwarf varieties also exist. *C. peruvianus:* from Peru, red-brown thorns; 'Monstrosus': has a bizarre shape; 'Nana': small variety. *C. chalybaeus:* intense blue.

CEROPEGIA WOODII
Rosary vine, String of hearts

The rosary vine, a tropical South African creeping and climbing plant of the milkweed family, has wire-thin shoots that grow to be as long as 2 metres (7 ft). Its artfully formed, tube-shaped blossoms end in five blackish-brown tips that bow towards each other, creating a sliding trap for insects; the plant blooms in the autumn. The rosary vine's fleshy, heart- or kidney-shaped leaves are marbled with silver on their top surface; round tubercles form on their axes in the summer; the root stalk is also tuberous. The rosary vine is ideally suited to hanging baskets, as a living curtain in a south-facing window, or as a trellis plant; it also grows well hydroponically.

The best location for a rosary vine will be bright or even sunny. It can live at room temperature throughout the year or be placed outdoors in the summer. Water moderately in the summer and sparingly when kept at lower temperatures in the winter; fertilise lightly in summer.

Re-pot in a porous substrate every two years.

Propagate via tubers or cuttings.

CHAMAEDOREA ELEGANS
Parlour palm

This extremely popular, delicate, thornless indoor palm with its elegantly hanging, feathery leaves originates in the humid mountain forests of Mexico and Guatemala. It is a dioecian plant and blooms even at a young age, bearing attractive, pale yellow flower axes. Its berry-like fruits are the size of peas.

The parlour palm prefers a bright to semi-shady location, but protected from direct sunlight. It should be kept at room temperature or outdoors in the summertime; in winter, it prefers temperatures around 15 °C (59 °F). Water regularly in summer and sparingly in winter; mist the plant frequently and occasionally immerse it when the summer days are very hot.

Fertilise lightly every two weeks in summer; re-pot in the spring, but only when absolutely necessary.

Propagates via seeds.

Other Species

Chamaedorea metallica remains smaller; *C. graminifolia* has long, narrow, feather-like leaves.

CHAMAEROPS HUMILIS
Mediterranean fan palm, European fan palm, Dwarf fan palm

The only palm native to Europe comes from the Mediterranean region. It is not quite as small as the name "dwarf" would imply: in the wild, it can be several metres high; in containers it grows more slowly and reaches a metre (3 ft) or so. The Mediterranean fan palm has a bushy growth pattern, and older plants develop a stem surrounded by brown filaments. Its shape is quite variable, and it blooms very infrequently, producing yellow panicles of flowers. It is a typical fan palm: its leaves stick up in a bushy formation and the leaf stems bear sharp thorns.

Place the Mediterranean fan palm in a sunny location outdoors from May to September; for the winter, it prefers a cool, airy and light room. Water and mist generously in the summer; in winter, water sparingly, depending upon the temperature. Supplement with liquid fertiliser every week in the summer. It is only necessary to re-pot the palm (in spring) if the roots have begun to grow out of the pot. Propagate via seeds.

> The Mediterranean palm is, on the whole, the least sensitive variety of palm. However, problems may arise in the form of spider mites, mealybugs or scale insects. The thorns on the leaf stems are quite capable of inflicting injury, so treat them with respect!

CHEIRANTHUS CHEIRI
Wallflower

The evergreen, perennial wallflower is a native of Asia and the Mediterranean region—particularly Italy and Greece. Not only is it a joy for the eyes with its gleaming flowers in warm shades of yellow, but its pleasant scent makes it a pleasure for the nose as well. The wallflower is a hardy and easy-to-care-for plant which begins blooming as early in the spring as temperatures allow. The wallflower loves full sun, but the soil should not be allowed to dry out after the seeds are sown. Water it generously in the summer, more sparingly in winter. When the weather becomes cold, take care that the root ball does not freeze. If you re-pot your wallflower in a new substrate in its second year, you will not need to fertilise it. Do keep children away from wallflowers, as they contain poisonous substances, particularly in the seeds.

Propagate via seeds or, in summer, via top cuttings.

Types

'Dwarf Goliath' grows to a maximum height of 30 cm (12 in); 'Goliath Giant' may grow to be twice as high, or 60 cm (24 in).

CHLOROPHYTUM COMOSUM
Spider plant, Ribbon plant, Hen and chickens, Airplane plant

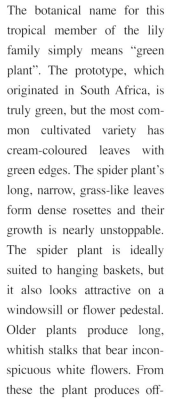

The botanical name for this tropical member of the lily family simply means "green plant". The prototype, which originated in South Africa, is truly green, but the most common cultivated variety has cream-coloured leaves with green edges. The spider plant's long, narrow, grass-like leaves form dense rosettes and their growth is nearly unstoppable. The spider plant is ideally suited to hanging baskets, but it also looks attractive on a windowsill or flower pedestal. Older plants produce long, whitish stalks that bear inconspicuous white flowers. From these the plant produces offshoots, bunches of young plantlets which can be rooted easily. The spider plant produces offspring tirelessly, so you can quickly collect a whole nest full of these green lilies.

The spider plant improves air quality in a room without demanding much: it grows all year long with no need for a rest period and does well in most conditions. It flourishes in warm rooms and cool ones, indoors as well as out. It tolerates light conditions from sun to semi-shade; however, if it is too dark, the contrasting leaf pattern will disappear.

Water normally to generously, depending on the air temperature. The plant enjoys an occasional misting if the air is dry. Fertilise weekly from March to September. Re-pot at the latest when the thick, water-retaining roots become visible at the top of the pot. Propagation is easy: detach the runner plantlets from the parent and set them in earth as soon as they have roots.

Types

The most familiar variety is 'Variegatum'; the newest type is green in the centre with cream-coloured edges.

CHRYSALIDOCARPUS LUTESCENS
Areca palm, Golden cane palm, Butterfly palm, Bamboo palm

This elegant, feathery palm from tropical Madagascar can reach up to 10 metres (33 ft) in its natural habitat; indoors it can grow to 2 metres (7 ft). Its form is bushy, with decorative, curving, comb-like feathered leaves. Even under artificial conditions, the areca palm will bloom after several years and develop attractive fruit axes. Older plants take on a golden, matured appearance; young plants develop above ground from the leaf sheaths.

The areca palm thrives in a moderately bright, warm (no less than 16 °C/61 °F) spot with high humidity—mist this plant generously. Keep the soil slightly moist; if the soil is warm, the plant will tolerate a footbath. Re-pot every two or three years. Propagate via seeds or offshoots.

> If an areca palm develops yellow leaves or brown spots on its leaves, this is a sign of over dry air. Winter heating, in particular, can lead to low humidity, which you can counteract by misting the palm frequently.

CHRYSANTHEMUM INDICUM
Chrysanthemum, Mum

In the past, these familiar composite flowers were available for All Saint's Day as a grave decoration to symbolise life. Now, thanks to cultivation under controlled daylight, they are available year round. The name chrysanthemum means "golden flower"; the plants originally come from China. These abundantly blooming plants, which blossom in the short days of autumn, are a longer-lasting alternative to cut flowers. There are varieties with large and small, simple and compound flowers, in every shade from white, yellow and orange to red and purple, in a wide range of shapes as well.

The mum's location should be bright, but not in direct sun. The flowers last longer in a cool spot. The plant may be placed outdoors from May. Keep the soil slightly moist at all times. Fertilise regularly, especially while flowering; remove wilted flowers immediately. It is not worth the effort to keep them over the winter.

Types

'Altgold': golden yellow, pompom shaped flowers, 40 cm (15 in); 'Purpur': pompom flowers, ca. 90 cm (3 ft); 'Weisse Nebelrose': pompom flowers, ca. 90 cm (3 ft); 'Anastatica': large purple flowers; 'Iowa': large yellow-orange flowers; 'Manito': azalea-like flowers.

CISSUS

Cissus, Grape ivy, Rex begonia vine, Tapestry vine

An old favourite among house-plants with many newly cultivated varieties is cissus, a member of the grape family.

It originates in the tropics and appears in many forms: there are climbing cissus plants and succulent cissus plants, and

even climbing succulents. Cissus is well suited to be a hanging or climbing plant, decorating trellises or room dividers.

Cissus plants like a bright to semi-shady location at room temperature. Kangaroo vine and grape ivy can also tolerate cooler temperatures in the winter. Water moderately with lukewarm water in the summer, less in winter depending on the temperature. Fertilise lightly from spring through mid-August; re-pot in the spring if necessary.

Propagate via cuttings at a soil temperature of 25 to 30 °C (77–86 °F).

Species and Types

Cissus antarctica, kangaroo vine: robust and fast-growing climbing evergreen shrub with shiny dark green, coarsely serrated leaves and reddish leaf steams and branches. *C. rhombifolia*, grape ivy, has three-part, diamond-shaped leaves; their top surface is shiny green while the underside is fuzzy and reddish; 'Ellen Danica' has more deeply notched leaves. *C. discolor* originates in Java: a hothouse plant; shiny, velvety leaves with a silvery olive green marbled pattern; leaf stems, branches and the undersides of the leaves are red; difficult to cultivate.

CITRUS

Miniature orange tree

These tropical and subtropical members of the rue family were introduced to the homes of European aristocrats in the Renaissance; they were cultivated in parks and orangeries. Their evergreen leaves have a leathery sheen; the pretty, fragrant blossoms are white; and the decorative little fruits often appear together with the blossoms. Miniature citrus trees usually grow to be 1 to 2 metres (3–7 ft) tall.

The miniature orange tree prefers bright and sunny conditions all year round: warm in summer and somewhat cooler (15–18 °C/59–64 °F) in

winter, but always bright. Water generously with softened water in summer; mist frequently. Water less often in winter. Fertilise lightly from March through August, and re-pot in spring if necessary. Citrus plants that lose their leaves in autumn should be kept cool and dry over the winter: they will usually develop new leaves in spring.

Propagation via cuttings is difficult; plants grown from seed will not usually blossom.

Species and Types

Citrus microcarpa, dwarf orange or calamundin from the Philippines, bears edible, bit-

ter little fruits which may be used for marmalade. *C. aurantium* 'Myrtifolia', chinotto or sour orange, bears wax-like white blossoms; the fruit is used for marmalade or juice. *C. taitensis* 'Otaheite' is a

dwarf variety from China. 'Fortunella japonica', a kumquat with edible oval fruit; crossing with *C. microcarpa* yields *Citrofortunella mitis*, calamundin orange, which may reach 1 or 2 metres (3–7 ft).

CLEISTOCACTUS

Silver torch cactus, Silver antlers, Cleistocactus

The South American silver torch cactus is a very unusual species. In its natural habitat, it grows in rocky areas with high humidity and can stretch up to 2 metres (7 ft). It is a columnar cactus with relatively narrow stems which branch out at the base and have multiple ribs. The white thorns grow densely and are so thin they almost resemble hair. Remarkable, too, are the tube-shaped flowers, which stick out from the sides of the plant like fingers; they open just wide enough for the style and the stamens to protrude.

The silver torch cactus thrives in a bright spot that's sunny in the summer (ideally outdoors) and cool in winter. It requires more humidity than other cacti, so mist it frequently with warm, soft water in the spring and summer. Keep the soil slightly moist at all times in summer, water sparingly in winter; re-pot in the spring if necessary.

Propagate via seeds or cuttings.

Types

Cleistocactus strausii, silver torch: originally from Bolivia, it has snow-white thorns, the flowers range from red-orange to scarlet. *C. baumannii:* produces abundant blossoms in colours from orange to scarlet. *C. smaragdiflorus:* flowers have bright red tubes with emerald green edges. *C. wendlandiorum:* has yellow and red flowers beginning when it reaches 15 cm (6 in).

> In order to encourage your silver torch cactus to grow, fertilise it once a week in the spring and summer.
> Use a special cactus fertiliser low in nitrogen.

CLERODENDRUM THOMSONIAE

Bleeding heart vine, Glory bower

This splendid member of the verbena family, a native of the African tropics, is a hardy creeping shrub and can spiral to heights of up to 4 metres (13 ft) in its natural habitat. Here in Europe, unfortunately, it is chemically treated and remains quite a lot smaller. The bleeding heart vine blooms during the rainy season. Its red flowers, which fall off quite quickly, are surrounded by long-lasting white sepals, which create an interesting contrast to the plant's dark green leaves.

The bleeding heart vine requires a warm, bright to semi-shady—but not sunny—location with very high humidity: a winter garden or enclosed plant window is ideal. The plant should have a two to three month rest period in a cool place in the winter: it will lose most of its leaves during this time.

Keep consistently moist with warm, soft water; water more sparingly during the rest period. Fertilise lightly once per week during the growth phase. Mist the plant frequently; it does not tolerate artificial heating. Prune and re-pot your bleeding heart vine at the end of February.

CLIVIA MINIATA
Kaffir lily, Clivia

This elegant member of the amaryllis family, originally from South Africa, is not a typical bulb plant. Rather, it has a bulb stem made of shiny, dark green, strap-like, evergreen leaves arranged on top of one another as pairs of leaf blades. A long flower stem rises between the leaves, bearing a magnificent umbel of 10 to 20 funnel-shaped blossoms. The red fruits that develop from these flowers cost the plant much strength. The Kaffir lily's roots are thick-skinned, and its leaves contain poisonous alkaloids.

Place your Kaffir lily in a bright to semi-shady spot with

plenty of fresh air. It can go outdoors in summer; in winter it needs to be kept cool. It needs complete rest from October to February, with temperatures of 10 to 12 °C (50–54 °F); water very sparingly. As soon as the flower stem is longer than 15 cm (6 in) water generously, but avoid standing water. Fertilise every two weeks from February to August. Re-pot after the blooming period—annually for young plants, less frequently for older ones.

Propagate using offshoots from the base of the plant; they should have at least four leaves when separated. You can also leave the offshoots on the parent plant and create entire "plant families".

Other Species and Types

'Citrina': creamy white flowers. *Clivia nobilis*: a smaller variety from the Cape Province.

COCOS NUCIFERA
Coconut palm

In its natural tropical habitat, the coconut palm is a tree, up to 30 metres (100 ft) tall with leaves as much as 6 metres (20 ft) long; it is one of the most important food plants in the tropics. Thanks to their fruit shells, coconuts can be carried great distances by the ocean and still germinate when they arrive on land.

The coconut palm—not to be confused with the miniature coconut palm or wedding palm (*Microcoelum weddelianum*)—requires a bright, warm, not too sunny but airy location; in winter, it appreciates extra light. Keep the soil slightly moist at all times with room-temperature water. Supplement with liquid fertiliser every two weeks from spring through autumn; re-pot as seldom as possible. Coconut palms do not reach old age in our homes, since the swimming vessel around the nut doesn't decompose as it does in the warm, moist tropics; instead, it hardens and hinders the young plant's growth. We also cannot offer the same great quantities of light available in the tropics. Propagation of coconuts is difficult.

CODIAEUM VARIEGATUM
Croton, Variegated laurel

The Southeast Asian croton is an evergreen shrub from the spurge family. Its shiny, asymmetrical, varied leaves display every colour from green through yellow to red. The pattern of its leaves varies, too: some are speckled, some marbled, some striped and some veined. Even young and old leaves on the same plant often look different from one another. The croton's flowers, however, are inconspicuous. The plant contains poisonous substances that irritate skin and mucous membranes.

Newer strains of crotons can even tolerate indoor condi-

tions when cared for diligently. The croton requires a bright location, but does not particularly like direct sunlight; the leaves will turn green if light is insufficient.

Room temperature and very high humidity are essential, as is warm soil; protect the plant from drafts.

Water your croton regularly and generously from March through September with soft, lukewarm water and fertilise weekly. Water the plant less in the winter, but mist it frequently. Re-pot in the spring if necessary—otherwise every one to three years. Mossing is the most successful method for propagation.

Species

Var. pictum is the only species, of which there are countless types.

COLEUS BLUMEI
Coleus, Painted nettle, Flame nettle

This colourful, tropical labiate is a relative of the stinging nettle. Its gorgeous leaves radiate in every colour from white and yellow through red and green to deep violet and

are fantastically patterned, striped, marbled and bordered. It is best to remove the inconspicuous flowers when they begin to bud. Coleus is an easy plant to cultivate.

Its location should be very light, even very sunny, since the interesting colours fade to green if it does not receive enough light. Keep the plant moderately warm, somewhat cooler in winter; it can even be in a sheltered location outdoors in the summer.

Water generously with soft water in the spring and summer, but do not drench the delicate leaves; keep only moderately moist in the winter. Supplement once a week with a lime-free fertiliser during the growing period; prune radically and re-pot in spring.

Propagate via cuttings in the summer or seeds in spring.

Species

Coleus pumilus: this is a dainty plant with small leaves which are red and white with green edges; makes a pretty hanging plant.

> Because of its attractive patterns and nettle-like leaves, coleus is sometimes called ornamental nettle. In reality, though, the visual appeal of this plant is short-lived: it already begins to fade in the second year and should make room a younger plant.

COLUMNEA
Columnea, Goldfish plant

This attractive gesneriad is native to tropical rain forests in Central America, where it grows in trees, allowing its long, flower-laden branches to cascade downward. Its striking, tube-shaped flowers are gleaming red to orange-red. Columnea is an ideal plant for a hanging basket.

Place columnea in a bright location where it is protected from drafts and direct sunlight. It requires a rest period at a temperature between 14 and 16 °C (57–61 °F) from December to January to re-stimulate flower production. Keep the soil consistently moist with soft, room-temper-

ature water; water less during the rest period. The plant needs to be supplemented with a lime-free fertiliser every week during the growth phase.

Prune and re-pot after the flowering period.

Propagate with cuttings bearing three pairs of leaves, planted in warm soil.

Species and Types

Columnea microphylla: small leaves; 'Stavanger': long branches; 'Hosta' and 'Variegata': variegated leaves. *C. hirta:* short, upright branches, red flowers up to 10 cm (4 in) long. *C. gloriosa* 'Purpurea': stunning variety, scarlet flowers. *C. banksii:* orange-red flowers.

CORDYLINE FRUTICOSA
Ti plant, Hawaiian ti, Cordyline, Good luck plant

These evergreen agaves originated in the tropical and subtropical regions of Austra-lia, New Zealand and East Asia. They are closely related to dracaenas, with which they are often confused. Ti plants can be identified by their thick, white, club-shaped roots. Their beautiful leaves are green, yellow, pink, red or multi-coloured.

The ti plant is excellently suited to hydroponic culti-vation. It requires a bright location without direct mid-day sun, high humidity and warm temperatures all year round. Its ideal home is an

enclosed plant window. Other varieties prefer cooler temper-

atures (5–10 °C/41–50 °F) in winter.

Water the ti plant generously in the summer, and less in winter depending upon the temperature; hothouse plants should be misted daily. Fertilise lightly every two weeks in the summer; re-pot in the spring if necessary.

Propagate via cuttings planted in warm earth; some other varieties are propagated via seeds.

Other Species and Types

Main species: dark green; 'Tricolor': green, red and yellow; 'Red edge': small and delicate. *Cordyline indivisa, C. australis, C. stricta:* re-frigerated glasshouse plants.

COREOPSIS GRANDIFLORA
Coreopsis, Calliopsis, Tickseed

Coreopsis, which originated in the Midwestern United States, can grow between 60 and 80 cm (24–30 in) high. From early summer until well into September, its bright yellow blossoms will conjure up a summer atmosphere on your balcony or patio.

The coreopsis is happiest in direct sunlight. Here, it requires an astonishing amount of water during the peak growing period: you will need to water it two to three times per day when temperatures are high. Fertilise moderately during the other periods. You will not need to fertilise for the first two months after potting; after that, fertilise every ten days. Coreopsis cannot survive over the winter and should therefore be treated like an annual plant.

Propagate via seeds, top cuttings or division.

> Since it is an annual, coreopsis does not require re-potting. Therefore, if the plant is housed in a container, it is all the more important that its roots be given enough room: make sure your pot is sufficiently large.

CRASSULA
Jade plant, Money tree

This South African member of the stonecrop or sedum family takes its name from the Latin *crassus* (fat), referring to the plant's fleshy leaves, in which it can store water. The leaves are opposite one another and the small blossoms are grouped on axes.

The jade plant is not demanding and easy to care for. It requires a bright, sunny spot, away from direct midday sun. In summer, you can place it outdoors where it is sheltered from rain; in winter, it prefers a cool (6–10 °C/43–50 °F) but nevertheless very bright location.

Water according to temperature. Keep the soil moderately moist in the summer, nearly dry in winter. The jade plant prefers dry air. Supplement with cactus fertiliser monthly in summer. Re-pot in spring, if needed, in sturdy pots.

Propagate via cuttings or seeds.

Species and types
Crassula arborescens, the familiar money tree, silver jade plant, Chinese jade: a tree-shaped plant, can grow very old and heavy, up to 1 metre (3 ft) high; leaves are mottled grey-white or shiny green, often with red edges; produces pink or white flowers after ca. ten years. *C. falcata*, scarlet paintbrush, propeller plant: whitish-grey leaves are slightly sickle-shaped and grow at an angle, fragrant red flowers; 'Morgan's Beauty' is especially pretty. *C. coccinea*, Rochee, formerly Rochea coccinea: many small opposing leaves in a cross; fragrant flowers in all shades of red; 30–60 cm (12–24 in) high. *C. ovata*; *C. argentea*; *C. corymbulosa*; *C. portulacacea*; 'Buddha's Temple' is a striking variety.

CROSSANDRA INFUNDIBULIFORMIS
Crossandra, Firecracker flower

This shiny-leaved, evergreen member of the acanthus family has its origins in India and Ceylon. Crossandra has attractive blooms which may be white, yellow, orange or red. In the past it was strictly a hothouse plant; now there are cultivated varieties suitable for growing in the home.

Crossandra's location should be bright (especially in winter) to semi-shady but protected from direct sunlight. The plant requires warm temperatures all year round—even in winter, temperatures should not go below 18 °C (64 °F)—as well as warm soil and very high humidity.

Keep the soil moist with soft, room-temperature water during growth and flowering periods; water less in winter. Fertilise weekly in summer; re-pot in spring prior to new growth. Propagate by planting cuttings in a heated propagating case; young plants need support. Seed propagation is also possible.

Types

'Mona Wallhed': a delicate variety with dark green, slightly wavy leaves; flowers are yellow, orange or salmon.

CTENANTHE
Ctenanthe

This member of the prayer plant family from the tropical rainforests of Brazil is cultivated for its abundant, beautifully patterned leaves. Its flowers are small, white and inconspicuous, but are still interesting to botanists due to their differentiated structure.

The ctenanthe flourishes best in a warm, moist plant window in a bright place, protected from direct sunlight. Both the air and the soil must be warm; even in winter, temperatures should not fall below 18 °C (64 °F).

Keep the soil moist with soft, room-temperature water. Be sure humidity remains high; mist several times a day if the plant is in a centrally heated room. Fertilise lightly every two weeks in summer. When needed, re-pot every two to three years in shallow containers with good drainage. Propagation works best via division.

Species and types

Ctenanthe oppenheimiana: the hardiest species; grows nearly 1 metre (3 ft) tall; leaf surfaces green with silvery-white stripes, undersides of leaves are purple. 'Variegata' has very distinct patterns; 'Tricolor' is irregularly speckled. *C. lubbersiana:* more delicate than others, 60 to 80 cm (24–30 in) tall; tops of leaves are marbled yellow and green, undersides light green. *C. kummeriana:* 40 to 60 cm (15–24 in) high; dark green leaves reddish underneath.

CYCLAMEN
Cylcamen, Persian violet

Cyclamen persicum, a member of the primrose family, is one of our most popular houseplants. Its charming, delicate blossoms, which are cultivated in many colours and shades, are similar to those of the plant's wild cousin. This prototype originally came from mountains of the eastern Mediterranean region. Cyclamen has attractive, heart-shaped, dark green leaves, usually patterned in silver-grey. It blooms from autumn to spring; most varieties have a rest period in the summer.

Do not throw the plant away when it has finished blooming, since they normally provide years of enjoyment.

Place your cyclamen in a cool, semi-shady place where it will receive fresh air: normal room temperature is too warm for this plant. It likes to be moist but not wet. It is best to water the plant from below in order to avoid wetting its extremely sensitive centre. You can pour out any excess water afterwards. Fertilise regularly, every week or two prior to and during the flowering period. Re-pot the plant in autumn, taking care not to cover the tuber with soil. Do not cut off wilted flowers or leaf stems, but pull them off with a firm tug or twist them. Propagation via seeds is possible, as is division of the tuber; however, both methods are usually unsatisfactory.

Types

There are numerous types of cyclamen, with white, pink, violet, red or salmon-coloured flowers. There are also fragrant, fringed and miniature forms.

CYMBIDIUM
Cymbidium orchid

The cymbidium orchid takes its name from the Greek kymbe ("boat"), a reference to its uniquely shaped lower lip. About 50 species of them grow from the Himalayas to Southeast Asia to Australia—on the ground, on rocks and in trees. They bloom in nearly every colour and provide the most cut flowers of any orchid variety; the cut blossoms keep for several weeks in water.

Depending on the species cymbidium orchids grow in refrigerated glasshouses or in hothouses; all varieties like very bright and airy conditions, warmer in summer and during the day than in winter or at night. Cold-loving plants may be placed in a semi-shady spot outdoors in summer. Water orchids generously during the growth period and supplement with special orchid fertiliser. As soon as the onion-shaped pseudobulbs have matured (usually in winter), put the plant in a cooler, drier location and withhold fertiliser. Re-pot ca. every three years. Propagate via division.

Hybrids

There are thousands of *Cymbidium* hybrids. In shops, you find the tall standard varieties and the popular miniatures, e.g. 'Agnes Norton', 'Show-off', 'Dag Oleste', 'Excalibur', 'Mary Pinchess', 'Del Rey', 'Miniatures Delight' (a hanging plant), 'Minneken', 'Pink Tower', 'Lemförde-Surprise'.

CYPERUS
Cyperus

These decorative sedges inhabit the swamps and riverbanks of tropical, subtropical and even some temperate regions. Pretty, umbrella-like tufts of long, mostly thin leaves sit at the end of the long, non-jointed reeds; in between are inconspicuous little umbels. The cyperus likes a bright to semi-shady spot, protected from direct midday sun. In summer it can go outdoors. In contrast to most other plants, "wet feet" are essential to the cyperus's survival. Particularly in summer, it needs to have water in its saucer: it needs to be kept very wet. (An exception is *Cyperus albostriatus*, which should not go outdoors in summer and does not like getting its feet wet.)

Humidity should be high, temperatures warm, somewhat cooler in winter. Fertilise lightly every week or two from April through August. Re-pot in the spring if necessary. Remove old stems regularly.

Propagate via leaf tufts that have taken root in water—or via division or seeds (the cyperus is a light-germinating plant).

Species and types

Cyperus alternifolius: 1 metre (3 ft) tall, slim with narrow leaves, 'Variegata' is white and coloured. *C. albostriatus:* wider leaves, often sold under the name *C. diffusus. C. gracilis,* dwarf papyrus: 30 cm (12 in) high. *C. haspan:* similar to papyrus, but 30 to 50 cm (12–20 in) high. *C. papyrus* was used by the ancient Egyptians for the manufacture of paper, mats and other products; three-cornered stems; fine, threadlike leaves which can grow to more than 2 metres (7 ft) in height.

CYRTOMIUM FALCATUM
Holly fern

The decorative holly fern, a member of the wood fern family, has its origins in East Asia, India and South Africa. Its dark green, fine-toothed fronds are single-feathered and feel leathery to the touch. The holly fern is undemanding and can even survive mild winters, buried in snow in a sheltered location.

Like most ferns, the holly fern loves high humidity and a cool, airy, shady to semi-shady location. Water generously in the summer with softened water; less in the winter. Place the plant out in the rain occasionally, mist, and immerse in water once a month. Fertilise lightly once a month in summer; re-pot in spring if necessary.

Propagates via spores or division.

Other Species and Types

'Rochfordianum': stronger and lovelier than the main variety; deeply notched plumes. *Cyrtomium caryotideum,* dwarf or fishtail holly fern: a pretty plant with delicate fronds, seldom available to purchase.

> The holly fern is quite an unproblematic plant. However, it has a tendency to fall victim to scale insect attacks. This fern is particularly suitable as a winter garden plant, since the conditions here are ideal to its growth.

DATURA SUAVEOLENS
Angel's trumpet

Almost no container plant attracts more admiring glances than the angel's trumpet. Its immense size—up to 4 metres (13 ft) tall—and its white, yellow, pink or orange-red flowers, which can grow up to 25 cm (10 in) long, recall the lushness of the tropics.

As one might guess, given that the plant's natural habitat is Central and South America, the angel's trumpet loves full sunlight, protected as much as possible from the wind.

In keeping with its size, the angel's trumpet requires a fairly large amount of water in the summer. You should not be too stingy with fertiliser, either: it requires additional nutrients every week up until the end of August. After that, it already begins preparing itself for winter, although it will continue to bloom until the first frost.

Good locations for wintering over—when the angel's trumpet needs only minimal watering—are a winter garden or a bright, cool cellar.

You can be quite bold when pruning in spring: angel's trumpet easily tolerates being cut back to one third its size.

Take special care if there are young children in your house,

as all parts of the angel's trumpet plant are highly poisonous.

Propagate by means of cuttings, from spring through late summer.

DAVALLIA
Hare's foot fern, Squirrel's foot fern, Davallia

This tropical fern, a member of the polypody family, has fresh green, finely jointed fronds and grows as an epiphyte. You can recognise this fern by its hairy, whitish to brownish rhizomes, which resemble hare's feet. The hare's foot fern feels most at home on an epiphyte stalk or a piece of bark; you can also tie its rhizomes around porous, water-filled clay pots. It is attractive as a hanging plant in a display case or a plant window.

The hare's foot fern requires high humidity, warm temperatures all year, and a bright, semi-shady location. Keep the soil uniformly moist with soft, room-temperature water. Mist frequently, fertilise lightly; re-pot only as necessary.

Propagate via division or spores. Keep the young plants moist and very warm.

Types

Davallia bullata is the most common species, originally from China. *D. mariesii, D. solida.*

The species most commonly found in our shops is the European *Davallia canariensis*, which takes its name from the Canary Islands. There, it stands out for its particularly luxuriant growth.

DICENTRA SPECTABILIS
Bleeding heart, Dutchman's breeches, Lyre flower

Seldom does a plant's name describe its appearance so perfectly as in the case of the bleeding heart. When its dark pink flowers open, they look exactly like hearts from whose point a single droplet is falling. The bleeding heart provides your balcony with a spectacular splash of colour in the spring and early summer, but dies off right after its flowering period, in May or June. During this time, you should take the opportunity to cut some of its decorative blooming branches for flower arrangements.

The roots of this fumitory are winter hardy, and excessive moisture will also scarcely hinder the plant's development. The bleeding heart prefers a moderately sunny to semi-shady location. Water it generously and take care to never allow the substrate to dry out. The damage that may result from a lack of water cannot be reversed. If you do not re-pot your plant, a single dose of fertiliser in spring is sufficient.

Propagation via division is rarely successful.

DIEFFENBACHIA
Dieffenbachia

One of the most popular foliage plants is the dieffenbachia, a member of the arum lily family native to American tropical rainforests. Its striking evergreen leaves are variously green, yellow-green and cream; striped and speckled. This tenacious, large-leaved plant, which gets up to 1.5 metres (5 ft) high, is recommended for larger rooms. As soon as it produces its inconspicuous flowers, which resemble those of the arum lily, its leaves begin to recede. For this reason, many people choose to remove the blossoms. Be careful: the dieffenbachia's juice is poisonous and irritating to the skin and mucous membranes. The dieffenbachia requires warm temperatures all year round, as well as high humidity and a bright to shady—but never sunny—location. It will not tolerate drafts or variations in temperature.

Water generously with lukewarm water in the growing period, moderately in the rest phase—preferably from below. Mist it regularly and wipe off with lukewarm water. The dieffenbachia is well suited to hydroponic culture. Fertilise sparingly every week or two in summer; re-pot every spring. Older plants may be pruned back in the early summer.

You can acquire top cuttings and stem sections from pruned stems; these can be cultivated in very warm soil.

Species and types

The *Dieffenbachia-Amoena* hybrids 'Tropic Snow' are particularly beloved as houseplants, with creamy-white marbled leaves ca. 60 cm (24 in) long. Also popular is *D. bowmannii* 'Camilla', whose light green patterned leaves grow up to 75 cm (30 in) long. *D. maculata* has white and green speckled leaves.

DIPLADENIA

Dipladenia, Mandevilla, Red Riding Hood

The name of this tropical South American member of the dogbane family means "double gland"; all parts of the plant are poisonous. The

delicate, slightly winding climbing shrub has thin branches, shiny green leaves, and large, beautiful, trumpet-shaped flowers which may be white, pink or purple. It looks particularly attractive growing on a trellis.

The dipladenia requires a bright but not sunny, very humid place at room temperature or warmer; 18 °C (64 °F) is adequate in the winter. Keep the soil consistently moist with soft, warm water from April through August and fertilise every one or two weeks. Water less after the blooming period is over. The plant needs a rest period in the winter; re-pot in the early spring.

Propagate via section cuttings planted in a heated propagating case.

Species and types

Dipladenia sanderi 'Rosea': large flowers, pink with yellow throats; 'Rubiniana': deep rose colour. *D. splendens*: flowers up to 10 cm (4 in) long, white outside with rose throats. *D. boliviensis*: white flowers with orange throats.

A tropical plant which prefers high humidity, the dipladenia will roll up its leaves if the air becomes too dry. Possible attacks of mealybugs or scale insects pose a threat to its health.

DIPTERACANTHUS

Dipteracanthus, Ruellia

These attractive tropical plants are natives of Brazil and, with approximately 250 species, they represent a large portion of the acanthus family. However, only a few of these species are available for purchase as houseplants, since they are somewhat difficult to cultivate.

In order for the plant to display the full glory of its delicate white-and-violet or pink flowers, it requires a warm and bright location, but it should not be placed in direct sunlight. In addition, you must ensure that the

humidity is high. A climate-controlled plant window can best meet these requirements. Water the dipteracanthus moderately with softened water, with which you should also occasionally mist its green and white leaves. If the soil is kept too moist, the plant can quickly fall victim to root rot. Supplement with low doses of fertiliser from April to August. Propagate the dipteracanthus via top cuttings in the spring or summer, making sure that the soil for the young plants is warm.

DIZYGOTHECA ELEGANTISSIMA
False aralia, Thread-leaf aralia, Spider aralia

This evergreen aralia, native to Australia and East Asia, is an elegant sight, capable of reaching 2 metres (7 ft) high. Its unique leaves are finger-shaped—initially tinged with red, later dark olive green and wider—gathered in clusters of 7 to 11 narrow, serrated leaves. False aralias like semi-shady conditions without sun, and warm air and soil temperatures throughout the year. An enclosed plant window at room temperature or warmer is the ideal location. Very high humidity is essential to false aralia's survival. Protect the plant from drafts;

it may take a rest period in the winter.

Water moderately but regularly, with lukewarm, softened water; water less in autumn and winter. Fertilise every two weeks from March to August. Mist the leaves liberally, particularly young plants. Re-pot young specimens each year; later, every two to three years.

Seed propagation is successful only when the seeds are very fresh.

Other Species and Types

Dizygotheca veitchii: wider, wavy leaves; 'Castor' is smaller and grows more compactly.

DRACAENA
Dracaena, Dragon tree, Corn plant, Ribbon plant

With approximately 40 tropical and subtropical species, the natural habitat of this lush member of the agave family ranges from the Canary Islands to Australia. Its name comes from Greek *drakaina* (female dragon). Its many green and coloured-leaved species are evergreen and grow into tall trees or bushes in the wild. Some varieties are palm-like, or resemble the ti plant (*Cordyline*), but they have yellow roots. Many species are hothouse plants, but some are suitable for a home or office.

The dracaena's spot should be bright (particularly for coloured-leaf varieties) to semi-shady, but away from the blazing sun. The plant likes to be warm all year round, but a cool winter rest period is possible. Humidity should be high; avoid drafts. Keep the soil consistently moist, drier if the plant is kept cool in winter.

Mist frequently and wipe the leaves with a damp cloth once per week. Fertilise every two weeks; re-pot young plants every year in April, older plants less often. Propagation: coloured varieties by cuttings; green types also via seeds.

Species and types

Dracaena marginata: from Madagascar; long, narrow leaves with reddish edges; 'Tricolor' is striped green, whitish and red, tolerates shade. *D. fragrans:* older plants have fragrant blossoms; 'Massangeana' and 'Victoria' are coloured-leaf varieties. *D. deremensis:* from East Africa; long, sword-shaped leaves, 'Warneckii'. *D. godseffiana* has an atypical appearance: shrub-like, speckled leaves, well suited to a plant window; can be propagated via division. *D. sanderiana:* leaf edges are yellow and white striped. *D. reflexa:* abundant growth; 'Song of India'.

ECHEVERIA
Echeveria, Plush plant, Hen and chicks

Echeveria is an easy-care member of the stonecrop family from the dry regions from northern California to southern Peru. It's named after Atanasio Echeveria, an 18th- century Mexican botanical artist. Its decorative, fleshy leaves grow in a spiral formation to form rosettes; they are often interestingly coloured, mottled or hairy. The bell- or pitcher-shaped flowers grow on umbels and may be white, yellow, orange, pink or red — or even multi-coloured. These charming little plants are long-lasting, even in dry indoor air, and take up very little space.

The echeveria likes a sunny, very bright spot, with dry air conditions. It prefers to be warm in summer — ideally in a stone garden. In winter it likes temperatures of 5 to 10 °C (41–50 °F); winter-blooming varieties somewhat warmer. Water sparingly in summer, even less in winter. Supplement with cactus fertiliser once a month from March to August. Re-pot in cactus soil in spring: annually for young plants; older plants every two to three years. Propagate via rosette offsets or leaf cuttings.

Species and types

Echeveria derenbergii comes from Mexico: mottled grey leaves with pointed tips, flowers are yellow to orange-red. *E. agavoides*: rust-coloured edges to leaves, 'Red Edge': brown, thorny tips. *E. carnicolor*: has flesh-coloured flowers; produces so many runners it can be kept as a hanging plant. *E. setosa*: leaves have white hair, red flowers with yellow tips. *E. nodulosa*: only 20 cm (8 in) high, red-edged leaves, red-brown flowers with yellow tips. *E. harmsii*: delicate, loosely-formed rosettes, rust-coloured flowers. *E. pulvinata*: white hairs; 'Ruby' has leaf edges that blend to red. *E. gibbiflora*: leaves have a waxy coating; bright red flowers.

ECHINOCACTUS
Golden barrel cactus, Pincushion cactus

These splendid thorny globes originated in Mexico, where they grow on the rocky terrain of highly elevated slopes, receiving the sun's strong rays during the day and cooling down at night. They store water, grow very slowly, and produce flowers on their woolly crowns only when mature.

This cactus needs a bright, sunny location with dry air. Protect it from direct sunlight only in spring, at the start of the growth period. Keep it very warm in summer; dry and bright in the winter rest period, at temperatures of 8 to 10 °C (46–50 °F). Water moderately during the growth period and supplement with cactus fertiliser ca. every two weeks. Re-pot only when necessary, being very careful of the plant's fragile roots. Propagation via seeds is difficult.

Species

Echinocactus grusonii, golden barrel, mother-in-law's seat: spherical, later columnar, grows up to 1 metre (3 ft) wide in the wild, very long-lived; sharp ribs with dense golden thorns, woolly crown; produces yellow flowers very rarely. *E. ingens*, large barrel cactus: according to legend, human sacrifices were performed atop this cactus; numerous ribs, yellow flowers.

E. horizonthalonius: round, flat, bluish-green, rose flowers.

ECHINOCEREUS
Hedgehog cactus, Strawberry cactus, Cup cactus

These sweet little cacti from Mexico and southwestern USA are column-shaped with fleshy stems which grow singly or branch out at the base; they may stand upright or lie on the ground. There are green and hairy species as well as

those with dense thorns. The scientific name is from Greek *echinos* (hedgehog). Most varieties are no more than 20 cm (8 in) tall. Their gorgeous flowers, in white, pink, red, purple and orange, usually with green stigmata, can be up to 12 cm (5 in) high.

The hedgehog cactus likes a bright location with full sun in summer, warm to hot temperatures and airy conditions; green varieties can also go outdoors. In winter the cactus requires a rest period in a sunny but cool and dry spot. Keep the soil somewhat moist in the summer; water green varieties more than those with

thick hair or thorns; keep dry in winter. Do not fertilise; plant in a porous, sandy substrate that contains some clay. Propagate via offshoots or using seeds.

Species

Echinocereus pectinatus: flowers range from white to pink; *var. rigidissimus:* thorn colour changes from white to red to brown; flowers are reddish with lighter throats. *E. salm-dyckianus:* orange flowers. *E. pentalophus:* light green with flowers up to 12 cm (5 in) high. *E. reichenbachii:* column-shaped, pink or purple flowers up to 12 cm (5 in) tall. *E. triglochidiatus:* winter hardy.

ECHINOPSIS
Sea urchin cactus, Easter lily cactus

These pretty, dark green, globe-shaped cacti originated in South America and are quite thorny. Their scientific name comes from the Greek *echinos* (hedgehog) and *opsis* (appearance). The attractive, funnel-shaped flowers may be white, pale pink, yellow or red; some bloom at night.

The sea urchin cactus prefers bright, airy conditions in the summer, protected from blaz-

ing sun: an outdoor location is ideal. Do not rotate. The plant requires a winter rest period in a cool, dry room. Water moderately in the summer and supplement with cactus fertiliser every three weeks; keep the plant completely dry in winter. Re-pot in winter if necessary. Propagate via offshoots or seeds.

Species and types

Echinopsis eyriesii: flowers up to 25 cm (10 in) long; greenish white, pleasant aroma. *E. oxygona:* very common. *E. aurea:* light yellow flowers; varieties include 'Peach Monarch' and 'Orange Glory'.

> Re-pot your sea urchin cactus only when necessary, every two to three years. Be sure to use a special cactus substrate, which is rich in nutrients.

EPIPHYLLUM
Orchid cactus

This tropical epiphyte's scientific name means "on the leaf", since its flowers arise out of flattened shoots which resemble leaves. The true leaves are nothing more than

tiny bristles. Orchid cacti bloom abundantly in radiant, beautiful colours ranging from white through yellow and red to violet. Most varieties bloom during the day, but night-blooming varieties also exist. In the rainforests, orchid cacti grow on the tops of trees; in our homes, they make very attractive hanging plants.

Give this popular cactus a warm, airy, bright location with high humidity, but away from direct sunlight. In the summer, it can even be placed in a protected spot in the garden. Avoid rotating the plant. It requires a rest period from November to February; keep the plant somewhat cooler during this time.

Keep the soil moderately moist with soft, room-temperature water; water less in winter; fertilise from March through August. Re-pot as infrequently as possible in humus, peaty soil.

Propagate via cuttings. Seed propagation is also possible.

Types

There are hundreds of types available, for example 'Gloria': pink-violet; 'Jennifer Ann': yellow; 'Pride of Bell': pale violet; 'M.A. Jeans': purplish-pink with white anthers; 'Mimi': a dwarf variety; the 'Falsche Königin der Nacht' blooms at night.

EPIPREMNUM PINNATUM
Pothos, Aureum, Devil's ivy

This tropical member of the arum lily family, a native of the Salomon Islands in the Pacific, has undergone a name change. Until recently it was known as *Scindapsus aureus*. The pothos is an undemanding climbing plant with leathery, often heart-shaped, somewhat asymmetrical leaves which are commonly striped or speckled in golden yellow or creamy white. In its natural habitat, it grows up the sides of trees to heights of several metres; but even in our homes the pothos is capable of covering entire walls with its branches. It makes an excellent hanging plant or a green decoration for room dividers or winter garden walls.

The pothos does not make any particular demands: place it in a semi-shady location at room temperature in warm soil. The plant should be kept

> The pothos likes to be misted frequently, since it feels particularly happy when the air is moist. All types also appreciate having their leaves washed from time to time.

somewhat cooler in winter, but it does not require a winter rest period.

Water evenly, a little less in the winter. Fertilise weekly from March through August; re-pot every two to three years. The pothos is very well suited to hydroponic culture.

Propagate via cuttings, which form roots very readily.

Types

Aureum: the most important variety; green and gold patterned leaves; 'Marble Queen': white and multicoloured, slow-growing, requires more light.

EUPHORBIA
Euphorbia, Spurge family

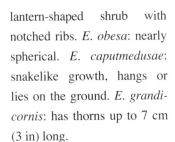

The widely varying spurge family originates in Africa: it includes shrub-like plants like the well-known crown of thorns, as well as cactus-like succulents with bizarre growing patterns—the "old world cacti". Their one common feature is their poisonous, milky juice—which irritates the skin and mucous membranes—and when they bloom their illusory flowers: coloured spathes which surround the actual blossoms.

A euphorbia's location should be sunny, bright and warm, only slightly cooler in the winter. It will also enjoy a protected location outdoors in summer; it tolerates dry air well. Water moderately, depending on the temperature, even less in winter; it is best to water the plant from below. Supplement with a little cactus fertiliser every two weeks. Crown of thorns requires a month's rest period after blooming. Re-pot in spring. Younger crown of thorns plants should be re-potted every year or two, older ones every three to four years in sandy substrate. Re-pot other species as necessary in cactus substrate.

Prune the plant in spring: cut-off sections may be used for propagation. Propagate via cuttings, allowing the cut edge to dry before planting.

Species

Euphorbia milii, crown of thorns: indestructible, bizarre, thorny shrub originally of Madagascar; blooms all year round; inflorescence with red, white, yellow or salmon-coloured spathes. *E. tirucalli*: thickly-growing shrub with pencil-thin branches; thrives hydroponically. *E. trigona*: lantern-shaped shrub with notched ribs. *E. obesa*: nearly spherical. *E. caputmedusae*: snakelike growth, hangs or lies on the ground. *E. grandicornis*: has thorns up to 7 cm (3 in) long.

EUPHORBIA PULCHERRIMA
Poinsettia, Christmas flower, Christmas star

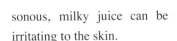

You see it everywhere in December: the poinsettia, a member of the spurge family from the mountainous regions of Mexico. Since it requires short days and long nights in order to bloom, it is easy to control its blooming period. What appear to be red, creamy white or salmon-coloured flowers are actually the upper brachts, which can last for several months: they surround the inconspicuous, short-lived true flowers.

You can continue to cultivate poinsettia after the holidays; it will develop into an attractive evergreen shrub. Its poisonous, milky juice can be irritating to the skin.

A poinsettia's location should be very bright, warm and free of drafts; the soil should also be warm. Water generously prior to blooming; fertilise weekly from June to October. Prune the plant back after it flowers, water more sparingly and place in a cooler location. Re-pot in mid-May.

Propagate using relatively long top cuttings.

Types

'Regina' has creamy white brachts; 'Gropom' is apricot-coloured; 'Dorothea' is a bushy, pink hanging plant.

EUSTOMA GRANDIFLORUM
Lisianthus, Prairie gentian, Texas bluebell

Lisianthus is a charming member of the gentian family, native to the prairies that extend of Nebraska, Texas and northern Mexico. Until recently, it was only familiar to Europeans as a cut flower. Although it grows up to 1 metre (3 ft) tall in the wild, it has been transformed into a sweet houseplant that stands 20 to 40 cm (8–15 in) high. Its wide, bell-shaped blossoms come in every colour from white to pink, violet to blue; its leaves are bluish-green.

The lisianthus requires a bright, but not sunny, and consistently warm location. Keep the soil moderately moist and fertilise lightly once a week. Unfortunately, it is not necessary to re-pot the plant, since it cannot be stimulated to bloom a second time. Under normal conditions, seed propagation is difficult.

EXACUM AFFINE
Persian violet, German violet, Tiddly winks

This pretty member of the gentian family comes from the island of Socrota in the Gulf of Aden, which is famous for its unique vegetation. It is not related to the impatiens, but it blooms just as abundantly and develops numerous branches. Its many small, mostly blue-violet flowers have a pleasant scent—all in all, a charming little plant.

The Persian violet is not particularly demanding: it likes warm, bright to semi-shady, airy conditions; you can place it outdoors in warm summer weather; protect it from drafts.

Water moderately but regularly; fertilise every two weeks. If you wish to cultivate the plant for a second year, re-pot it in spring.

Propagate in the spring via cuttings, or in February via seeds: do not cover the seeds with soil.

> The Persian violet is a light-germinating plant, meaning it is essential that the seeds receive light in order to sprout. Therefore, when you sow the seeds in January or February, do not cover them with soil. Cuttings should be made in spring. They are particularly happy when planted in cultivation soil.

FATSHEDERA LIZEI
Aralia ivy, Bush ivy, Fat-headed Lizzy, Tree ivy

This attractive aralia is not actually a species, but a cross between an ivy and an aralia. It was cultivated in 1912 at the Lize-Freres tree nursery in Nantes. Its evergreen leaves, which have three to five lobes, are similar to the aralia's, but longer and harder. The plant has its long tendrils and its desire to climb from the ivy. Aralia ivy initially grows slender and upright, but after it reaches a certain height it requires a climbing support. It is robust and tolerates shade; it is also an ideal graft base for high-stemmed ivies.

Aralia ivy's location should be bright (colourful varieties) to shady with plenty of fresh air. It likes room temperature in the summer, with somewhat cooler nights; it should be kept cool in winter. Keep the soil slightly moist; water less in winter; fertilise every two weeks in summer. Re-pot young plants every year in the spring, older ones only as needed. Prune the plant back when re-potting to allow it to develop a bushier shape.

Propagate in the summer via cuttings.

Type

'Variegata': white and multi-coloured, grows more slowly.

> This hardy cross between a fatsia and an ivy can grow up to 5 metres (16 ft). Support the plant regularly to ensure that it maintains an attractive, bushy shape: otherwise, it tends to lose its lower leaves.

FATSIA JAPONICA
Fatsia, Japanese aralia

This thickly growing, evergreen aralia from Japan can grow up to 2 metres (7 ft) tall indoors, and is named for the Japanese word for the number eight. In fact, its hand-shaped, deeply notched leaves have seven to nine lobes. They are shiny and leathery on the surface, matte on the underside and grow up to 40 cm (15 in) wide. The fatsia's small white umbel flowers develop into bluish-black berries.

The fatsia likes a bright to shady location away from direct sunlight; it prefers to be cool all year round. Keep the soil moderately moist; water less in winter, depending on the temperature. Fertilise every week in the summer; re-pot in the spring only if the roots are completely pot-bound.

Propagate via seeds, cuttings or mossing.

Types

'Variegata' and 'Albomarginata' have coloured leaves; 'Reticulata' has a net-like pattern. 'Maserie' is stocky with larger leaves.

FAUCARIA
Tiger's jaw

The South African tiger's jaw is a very decorative little plant in the fig-marigold family. Its fleshy leaves, which may have few or many teeth, are arranged opposite one another in pairs so that they resemble a tiger's open jaws. The leaves are sometimes patterned in white. Tiger's jaw is a low-growing plant that forms a lawn or ground cover. It blooms beginning in August, bearing large, dazzling yellow flowers.

In the summer, tiger's jaw will thrive in a warm and airy location that receives full sunshine—preferably outdoors; in the winter, it prefers a cool, dry room. Water it generously in the summer; keep the soil dry during the rest period. Repot the plant about every three years.

Propagation takes place via seeds or cuttings.

Types
Faucaria tigrina, tiger's jaw: green leaves speckled with white, long, thin teeth around the edges; grows up to 15 cm (6 in) tall. *F. felina*, cat's jaws: yellow or orange flowers. *F. lupina*, wolf's Jaw.

Tiger's Jaw makes an ideal houseplant, since its flowers spring up almost by themselves. Its seeds behave in a similar fashion: sow them in a sandy, part-clay and humus substrate. When moistened with a little water, the seeds will then grow just as they do in the desert conditions of their home.

FELICIA AMELLOIDES
Blue marguerite, Blue felicia, Kingfisher daisy

This particularly delicate and filigreed species of daisy originates in the southern regions of Africa. It flourishes inside the house as well as outdoors; however, it requires direct sunlight in both locations. Its blue, violet or white flowers will not open if they are not exposed to the sun. Even the seeds require so much light in order to germinate that it is best to simply strew them over the surface of the soil.

Do not skimp on water for this plant in the summer; water twice a day when the weather is hot. A dose of fertiliser every two weeks is also essential.

If you keep these plants over the winter, be sure to prune them radically in spring so that they will maintain a compact appearance later on.

Propagate via seeds (in the summer for winter blossoms indoors; in the spring for summer flowers) or top cuttings in the summer (to obtain blossoms indoors in the late autumn).

Other Species and Types
Felicia bergeriana, F. tenella. 'Blue Daisy' is light blue with a golden eye, 30 cm (12 in) tall.

FICUS
Ficus, Weeping fig

The many evergreen members of the mulberry family, originating in the tropics and subtropics, differ widely in appearance: they may be trees or shrubs, climbing or hanging plants. All of them produce a non-poisonous, milky sap which contains latex; their flower structure, pollination and fruit formation are unique in the plant kingdom. Approximately 20 species of this family have become well-loved houseplants.

The classic example is the ever-popular rubber tree: it has shiny, green, oval leaves approximately 30 cm (12 in) long; the younger leaves are encased in a red stipule.

The ficus likes a bright to semi-shady location with a constant room temperature; avoid drafts and changes in location. Coloured-leaf varieties require more light than green ones; hydroponic cultivation is also possible. Water the plant with lukewarm water: moderately in the spring and summer, more sparingly in the winter, depending upon the species. Keep the soil warm. Mist the ficus frequently, wipe off smooth leaves with a damp cloth. Fertilise every two weeks in the spring and summer; re-pot in spring if necessary. Pruning will usually encourage branch development.

Propagate in spring via cuttings planted in a heated propagating case; or via mossing in the summer.

Species and Types

Ficus elastica, rubber tree: 'Decora' has dark green, 'Doescheri' variegated leaves. *F. benjamina,* weeping fig: delicate leaves, overhanging branches; coloured varieties also exist, e.g. 'Variegata'. *F. lyrata,* fiddle-leaf fig, banjo fig: well suited to large rooms. *F. pumila,* creeping fig: climbing or hanging branches, clinging roots, excellent for hanging baskets. *F. deltoidea*: epiphytic, slow-growing with pea-sized yellow green pseudocarps.

FUCHSIA
Fuchsia

The fuchsia, a member of the nightshade family, is named for 16th-century doctor and botanist Leonhard Fuchs. Its prototypical species live in the cool, moist mountain forests of Central and South America, the Falkland Islands and New Zealand. Fuchsias are commonly known as balcony and container plants; in recent years, many varieties for indoor growing have been cultivated. The plant's graceful blossoms can be found in every shade from white to pink and red to blue. Plants are available with tiny or large, single or compound, bell-shaped or tube-shaped, single- or bi-coloured flowers. There are upright as well as hanging fuchsia varieties.

The fuchsia's location should be semi-shady and moder-

ately warm. The plants like to be outdoors in the summer; in winter, they prefer bright and cool conditions at 5 to 15 °C (41–59 °F). Keep the soil uniformly moist, water according to temperature; the air should not be allowed to become too dry. Fertilise weekly in the summer; prune back and re-pot in the early spring.

Propagate via cuttings.

Types

Single-flowered fuchsias, e.g. 'Tolling Bell', 'Winston Churchill'. Compound-flower varieties include 'Dollarprinzessin': red calyx, red and blue crown. Hanging fuchsias: 'Pink Galore' has compound, dusty rose flowers; 'La Campanella'. *Triphylla* hybrids: extra long, tube-shaped flowers; 'Gartenmeister Bonstedt': salmon-orange colour.

GARDENIA JASMINOIDES
Gardenia, Cape jasmine

The gardenia, a member of the East Asian coffee family, is an evergreen, luxuriously branching shrub with glossy, dark green leaves, which can grow up to 1.5 metres (5 ft). Its fragrant, creamy white flowers can grow up to 10 cm (4 in) wide. Gardenias were widely used as boutonnieres or corsages in the 19th century. Today, these elegant plants are cultivated as pot plants or cut flowers.

The gardenia requires bright conditions all year round: a winter garden is ideal. It can also be placed outdoors in good summer weather; keep it from direct sunlight. Conditions should be consistently warm in summer, 15 to 18 °C

(59–64 °F) in winter, but in warm soil. The gardenia is difficult to care for. Keep the soil uniformly moist with sof-tened, room-temperature water, avoid standing water. The plant requires high humidity, but refrain from misting as soon as the blossoms appear. Supplement with lime-free fertiliser (azalea fertiliser) once a week during the growing and blooming periods; re-pot every three years in spring.

Propagate in the spring or late summer, taking top cuttings without flowers; plant them in a heated propagating case.

Types

'Fortunei' and 'Veitchii' are attractive compound varieties.

GASTERIA
Gasteria, Ox tongue

These unusual succulents are native to South Africa and at first glance not recognisable as members of the lily family. Their fleshy leaves are usually arranged in double rows, less frequently in a spiral form. They are tongue-shaped with warty or speckled surfaces. The brown-red, bell-shaped blossoms sit on loose flower axes on a long stalk.

The gasteria appreciates a warm, sunny location; it also tolerates shade, but will not produce flowers if placed there. Move it to a cooler location in winter, at tempera-tures of 10 to 15 °C (50–59 °F). Keep the soil moderately moist; fertilise lightly in summer. Re-pot the plant as needed in shallow containers. Propagates via offshoots.

Types

Gasteria verrucosa, ox tongue: has leaves in double rows with pearly warts. *G. pulcher* has speckled leaves.

> You can propagate this plant via leaf cuttings, but the cut-off edge of the leaf you remove must be allowed to dry completely before it is set in a pot filled with somewhat sandy, part-clay soil.

GAULTHERIA PROCUMBENS
Wintergreen, Canada tea, Partridge berry, Boxberry

The wintergreen, which originally comes from North America, is an ideal plant for the patio or balcony. It is a member of the heather family—and like heather it does not tolerate lime well, be it in the soil or the water. The plant's leaves fade to yellow if exposed to it. In spring and summer, the wintergreen displays a multitude of white to pale pink flowers, from which its gleaming red berries will develop in the autumn. The plant's leaves also change colour, taking on a reddish tone in the colder months.

The wintergreen is completely winter hardy. When temperatures are below freezing, you simply need to keep the roots moist. In summer, it requires a great deal more water.

The wintergreen is also undemanding as far as its location is concerned. It will grow anywhere except in a place that is shaded all day long. It appreciates an occasional dose of a fertiliser that contains potassium.

Propagate via semi-mature cuttings in summer or seeds in the autumn. The wintergreen's abundant roots make division a particularly easy option.

Other Species

Gaultheria itoana, G. miqueliana, white flowers and pale pink or white berries; *G. shallon.*

GERBERA X JAMESONII
Gerbera, African daisy, Transvaal daisy, Barberton daisy

The evergreen gerbera, native to South Africa, is not a plant that can live outdoors all year round: it should never be exposed to frost. However, if it is allowed to migrate between indoor and outdoor locations, it will bloom throughout the summer. Its large flowers come in colours from white and yellow to dusty rose and red shades. Its lovely blossoms make the gerbera one of the best-known cut flowers.

Although the gerbera can happily tolerate full sunlight outdoors in the summer, you must protect it from direct rays while it is in the house.

Water only sparingly in winter, and place the plant in a cool place. In summer, on the other hand, the soil should be kept moist (use lime-free water) and it should be fertilised every two weeks. It is easy to propagate the gerbera, either using seeds or via division.

Other Species

Gerbera viridiflora.

GREVILLEA ROBUSTA
Silky oak

This pretty, tropical member of the protea family is evergreen, undemanding and fast-growing. In its native Australia it can grow 50 metres (165 ft) tall; in our homes it is a delicate indoor tree of 1 to 3 metres (3–10 ft). The silky oak is no relation to the oak tree. Its magnificent flowers never appear in home cultivation: they only develop on older plants. Its feathery leaves have a silvery shimmer early in their growth and resemble fern fronds.

The silky oak likes a semi-shady location protected from blazing sun; it can also live outdoors in summer. Keep the plant cool in the winter, warm in summer. Keep the soil uniformly moist; water less in winter depending on the temperature. Fertilise weekly in summer; re-pot in spring if needed. Propagate in spring, using fresh seeds sown in warm (20 °C/68 °F) sawdust.

> Aphids are an issue when cultivating a silky oak. In addition, the plant reacts strongly to improper conditions: if fertiliser is lacking its leaves will fade in colour. If the roots are too dry or too wet the leaves fall off. Over-warm temperatures will cause the plant to grow too quickly.

GUZMANIA
Guzmania

The guzmania, a flamboyant member of the pineapple family, comes from the tropical rainforests of South America. Its long leaves form rosettes up to 50 cm (20 in) in height and width, in which the plant collects rainwater. Its striking, usually bright-red spathes form a strong contrast with the surrounding leaves and last several months—much longer than the actual flowers.

Guzmania is happiest in an enclosed plant window or hothouse, either in a flowerpot or secured to an epiphyte stalk. Here, the conditions should be bright to semi-shady, warm in spring and summer, and at least 18 °C (64 °F) during the rest of the year; humidity should be high. Water and mist generously with soft, room temperature water during the growth period; water less in winter.

Water the guzmania into its leaf funnel: the plant will absorb the water through its trichomes. Fertilise lightly every two weeks from March through August. There is no need to re-pot, since the guzmania will only bloom once from each funnel and then die off. However, the plants often form offshoots at the base of the parent plant.

Propagation via offshoots; they require approximately two years to produce flowers.

Species and Types

Guzmania hybrids include 'Internedia' and 'Magnifica', whose scarlet spathes last for more than six months. *G. minor*: leaf rosettes grow to about 20 cm (8 in) wide; white flowers.

GYMNOCALYCIUM
Gymnocalycium, Chin cactus

These unusual South American spherical cacti are well known to all cactus lovers. They bear stunning white, yellow, pink or red flowers, which are often larger than the plant itself. Since 1941 chlorophyll-free coloured varieties have been cultivated in all shades from yellow to red. These non-green cacti cannot live on their own; they must be grafted to green base plants in order to bloom.

The gymnocalycium likes a bright and airy spot, but protected from direct sunlight. It likes warm conditions in summer and may be placed outdoors. In winter keep it at 8 to 10 °C (46–50 °F); the cactus tolerates dry indoor air well.

Water moderately in summer and feed occasionally with cactus fertiliser. In winter, water just enough that it doesn't dry out. Re-pot in nutrient-rich, porous cactus substrate.

Propagate via seeds or off-shoots; coloured offshoots must be grafted.

Species

Gymnocalycium mihanovichii: chlorophyll-free, red, cultivated in Japan; the starting form for the "moon cactus" or "ruby ball". *G. denudatum,* spider cactus: spider-like thorn formation, has white to red flowers up to 5 cm (2 in) tall. *G. gibbosum:* blue-green with beautiful white to pink flowers. *G. andreae*: sulphur-yellow flowers. *G. quehlianum*: white flowers on red ground.

GYPSOPHILA MURALIS
Baby's breath

Baby's breath, a plant native to Europe, is a popular choice for giving stability and form to flower arrangements with its long, narrow little leaves and countless small, white or pale pink flowers.

Baby's breath can add colour to your window boxes in the late summer and autumn, when other plants are already beginning to prepare for their rest periods.

You will normally find baby's breath for sale in shops as a complete plant: its seeds may be difficult to come by in some areas.

Baby's breath is usually intended as an annual plant; it is not winter hardy. The best location for this plant is in direct sunlight.

Water moderately; do not allow the surface of the soil to dry out. In principle, baby's breath is not a sensitive plant and can even tolerate water that contains lime. Wait to fertilise for six to eight weeks after re-potting; after that, fertilise every ten days.

HAWORTHIA
Haworthia, Zebra plant

The extensive lily family also includes succulent varieties. One is the South African haworthia, which grows in a variety of shapes with its fat, fleshy leaves arranged in rosette formations. Most species of haworthia have white, pearly warts on the dark undersides of their leaves. Some species hide themselves almost completely under the ground—for example, *Haworthia truncata*, of which only the chlorophyll-free "windows" remain visible.

The regular, pearly-leaved species like a very bright, but not sunny location that is warm in summer. Water moderately in the summer and fer-

tilise every four weeks. The plant requires a rest period from October to February, at temperatures of 10 to 12 °C (50–57 °F); keep it nearly dry. The "window" species should be placed in a hothouse or an enclosed plant window with bright and sunny conditions. Keep slightly moist in winter, at 14 to 16 °C (57–61 °F); during the rest period, from April through September, keep the plant drier and do not fertilise.

Avoid standing water with all species. Re-pot approximately every two years in spring. The window varieties require a somewhat heavier substrate than the other species.

Propagate by separating offshoots or via seeds.

Species

Haworthia fasciata: the best-known species, it has white warts joined together in horizontal lines. *H. glabrata:* closely studded with pearl-like, white knobs. *H. attenuata:* its warts form white, horizontal lines. *H. reinwardtii:* has warts that are arranged in vertical and horizontal lines.

HEBE ANDERSONII
Hebe

There are about a hundred species of this evergreen member of the figwort family, which originates in New Zealand, Australia and New Guinea. Its tube-shaped

flowers grow in clusters, ears or little balls and may be white, pink, blue, purple or red.

The hebe makes a good potted plant, but it is equally suitable for planting in hedge borders or stone gardens. However, you should only do this if you live in a mild climate: the plant needs to be protected from cold, drying winds in winter.

Plant the hebe in moderately fertilised potting soil that contains clay; water only

lightly during the growing period. A monthly dose of liquid fertiliser is sufficient.

Indoors, the plant likes a well-lit location; it can also easily tolerate full sunlight.

Prune the hebe back in the autumn, after the blossoming period.

It is possible to propagate via cuttings taken from October through December. Re-pot them once they have taken root; you can plant them outdoors beginning in mid-May.

HEDERA HELIX
Ivy, English ivy

Of our few native house-plants, the familiar, beloved ivy has been a companion to humans since olden times. It is an evergreen, climbing shrub which can grasp overhanging walls with its root-like fibres. Its leaves—which may be dark green or patterned in white, depending on tvariety—are usually lobed; but leaves on fruit-bearing branches are not lobed. The ivy's berries contain poisonous substances. Ivy makes an excellent hanging plant; it is also well suited for decorating walls, as a winter garden plant, or as a ground cover in large containers.

Ivy's location should be cool, particularly in winter (some varieties can survive winter outdoors): green-leaved varieties like shadier and cooler conditions. The more colourful the leaves, the brighter and warmer it should be.

Water moderately in summer, less in winter. Fertilise lightly once per week in summer. Re-pot ivy every year; prune back any balding branches.

You may propagate the plant via cuttings all year round.

Type

Hedera canariensis 'Variegata': taller than *H. helix*, large leaves patterned in white, likes warm conditions all year.

HELIOTROPIUM ARBORESCENS
Heliotrope

The most striking feature of this annual plant that hails from Peru is its intense vanilla aroma. From early summer until well into autumn, its umbels are a true pleasure for everyone who loves blue and violet colours. Although the heliotrope is a sun-worshipper, it actually flourishes best under a protective roof. There, it is sheltered from blazing sun as well as rain. The heliotrope is one of the few patio plants whose flowers can be destroyed by rain. During the growth period, the plant requires a relatively large amount of water; water moderately at other times. Fertilise every two weeks.

Propagate via seeds or cuttings in the summer or early autumn.

Types

'Mini Marine' has gorgeous blue-violet flowers and grows to ca. 30 cm (12 in). 'Marine' has flowers of the same colour, but is ca. 60 cm (24 in).

The heliotrope's aromatic vanilla fragrance also seems to attract other creatures: white flies hide between the folds on the undersides of the plant's leaves. If you look closely, you can spot flies, eggs and nymphs, all of which should be combatted immediately.

HEMEROCALLIS
Daylily

The daylily, a member of the *Liliaceae* family, owes its somewhat unusual name to the fact that its yellow, trumpet-shaped flowers open for only a single day. This situation sounds sadder than it actually is, since this plant is a particularly industrious producer of blossoms and sends out new flowers continually. The daylily has only limited appeal as a cut flower, since you must take care to cut the stems precisely when the blooms are in the bud stage to ensure that they will open in a vase.

The daylily produces flowers most intensively when it is placed in direct sunlight, although it should be protected from the harsh midday sun. The pleasantly fragrant daylily is a winter-hardy plant, which likes to spend its rest period in a frost-free location. Water regularly and fertilise once per month. Re-pot every three to four years.

Propagate via division after the blooming period.

Species

Hemerocallis aurantiaca: dark orange flowers. *H. citrina*: light yellow flowers.

H. dumontieri, H. fulva, H. middendorffii: all with orange flowers; *H. minor*: all these have yellow flowers.

HIBISCUS ROSA-SINENSIS
Hibiscus, Rose of China, Rose mallow

This magnificent member of the mallow family is thought to originate in south China. It bears wide, funnel-shaped flowers which can be up to 15 cm (6 in) tall, with long, protruding stamens. Each blossom lasts just a day, but new ones constantly replace the old. Many varieties are available in brilliant colours, ranging from white to yellow, orange, salmon-coloured, pink and red—you can even find two-toned flowers. There are single, double and compound-flower varieties; the compound blossoms last somewhat longer. The plant's glossy leaves are evergreen.

The hibiscus loves a warm, bright location; you can even place it outdoors in summer. The plant normally blooms from May through the late autumn. It is best to give it a rest period in a somewhat cooler location in winter.

Water generously during the main vegetation period, and fertilise once per week; water less in the winter. Mist the plant frequently if placed in a heated room. Do not rotate! Prune and re-pot the hibiscus in the early spring: every year for younger plants, older ones less often.

Propagate in spring using semi-mature top cuttings.

HIPPEASTRUM
Amaryllis, Potted amaryllis, Dutch amaryllis

The hippeastrum, a member of the amaryllis family, is native to South and Central America—specifically, the areas that have a distinct dry season. A tall, hollow stalk arises from the plant's large bulb and produces two to four enormous, brilliantly coloured, funnel-shaped flowers with prominent yellow stamens. The hippeastrum's leaves appear at the same time as the flower or shortly afterwards. The plant contains poisonous substances. The bulbs, which are sold primarily during the Christmas season, are planted in such a way that the upper third protrudes out of the soil. Water the bulb sparingly and place it in a bright or sunny location. As soon as shoots appear, water somewhat more liberally; place in a cooler location during the blooming period. Water generously after the flowering period and fertilise once a week during the period of leaf growth, up through the month of August. This is critical for the production of flowers in the following year. Always water with soft, room temperature water; be sure that the pot has good drainage. Remove dry leaves in the early autumn; allow the bulb to rest in a dark place at 15 to 18 °C (59–64 °F).

Propagation is most successful using apple-sized bulblets.

Hybrids

These plants are sold almost exclusively as hybrids, e.g., 'Apple Blossom': pink and white, delicate fragrance; 'Fantastica': red with white stripes; 'Dutch Belle': deep pink; 'Ludwig's Goliath': fiery red; 'Fairyland': pink. White varieties include 'Maria Goretti', 'Ludwig's Dazzler', 'Picotee', 'Early White'.

HOYA
Hoya, Wax flower, Porcelain flower

This pretty, evergreen climbing plant is named after English gardener Thomas Hoy. The genus *Hoya*, which comprises ca. 200 species, comes from the belts of land between East India, South China and Australia; we are familiar with two species here in Europe. Both bloom in summer, bearing waxy, star-shaped, milk-white flowers with red centres. Many blossoms are clustered together on overhanging umbels which turn towards the light. Particularly late in the day, the flowers emit a sweet fragrance, and in warm weather they sometimes secrete a sweet, honey-like nectar.

Hoya carnosa, the large wax flower, has thick, fleshy leaves and develops pliable branches which may be several metres long; it can live to a very old age. It is best to cultivate the wax flower as a creeper, on a trellis or surrounding a window. *Hoya bella* is more delicate and flourishes best as a hanging plant.

The hoya likes bright to semi-shady conditions at room temperature or warmer; it tolerates dry interior air well. However, you should protect the plant from the scorching midday sun, from drafts or drastic changes in temperature. *Hoya carnosa* prefers to be somewhat cooler in the autumn and winter; *Hoya bella* is a heat-loving species. Do not change the plant's location once it has started to form buds! Water moderately from the bud stage until after the flowering period; simply keep the plant moist during the rest period. Mist regularly during the blooming period, and fertilise only every 24 weeks. Re-pot only very infrequently and very carefully. In the case of *Hoya carnosa*, be sure to leave its short flower stalk standing: it will develop new blossoms.

> This houseplant, with its sometimes intoxicating fragrance, does not appreciate a change of location once it has begun to produce buds. If you move it, it is likely to react by losing its flowers.

HOWEIA
Kentia palm

The Kentia palm grows only on Lord Howe Island, located east of Australia. The island's capital city is Kentia, from which the plant gets its name. It has become one of the most popular indoor palms, and is available in a wide range of sizes. It is both decorative and tolerant of dry interior air. Its elegant, overhanging leaves are evenly feathered and strongly veined. The Kentia palm has a long lifespan and with time, can grow up to 2.5 metres (8 ft) tall.

The palm's location should be shady to semi-shady (in the wild, the young plants grow in the shadow of larger trees).

Older plants may be placed in a protected spot outdoors in summer. The Kentia palm prefers to be at room temperature throughout the year, somewhat cooler at night and in the winter.

Water this palm at regular intervals with soft, room temperature water, somewhat less in winter; avoid standing water. Fertilise weekly in summer. Re-pot in a deep container, as infrequently as possible.

Species

Howeia forsteriana: grows faster and wider; larger leaf fronds. *H. belmoreana*: has slow-growing, upward-sprouting leaves.

HYACINTHUS ORIENTALIS
Hyacinth

This beloved, spring-blooming member of the lily family originated in the Mediterranean region and Asia Minor. Its fragrant blossoms, which stand in upright clusters, can be found in a rainbow of shades from white through yellow and red to blue. The 'Multiflora' variety is one that produces several flower stalks per bulb.

You can cultivate the bulbs yourself: plant them in evenly moist soil, usually in autumn, or on a growing container filled with soft water, about 2 mm (less than $1/8$ in) above the water. They will require eight to ten weeks in the dark, at temperatures below 12 °C (54 °F), in order to develop roots. Cover the shoot with a small hood until it pushes it away by itself. Make a careful transition to a bright room and moderate warmth.

Types

'L'Innocence', 'Aventine Arendsen' and 'Edelweiss' have white flowers. Some pink-flowered varieties include 'Anne Marie', 'Pink Pearl', 'Amsterdam' and 'La Victoire'. 'Delfts Blau' and 'Osatera' are blue; 'Tubergens Scarlet' and 'Jan Bos' red; and 'City of Harlem' is yellow.

> You can also cultivate hyacinths in pots. If you would like to decorate your living room with flowers in December, plant the bulbs in the soil in September or October and cover them with an extra layer of sand.

HYDRANGEA MACROPHYLLA
Hydrangea, Hortensia

The hydrangea, a member of the saxifrage family, originates from Japan. Its botanical name means "water vessel"; macrophylla means large-leaved. The hydrangea loves to be outdoors, where it can grow into a 4-metre (13-ft) tall shrub in an ideal location. It will also grow indoors for shorter periods of time. In spring and summer the hydrangea develops luxuriant, spherical inflorescence; it takes a rest period in autumn and winter. What appear to be flower petals are actually sepals; the true flowers are very inconspicuous.

The soil's acid content has a strong influence on the colour of the hydrangea's flowers. Their original colour is red: blue flowers can be produced from pink or red varieties by adding acid to the soil. White hydrangeas also exist. Hydrangeas prefer cool, bright to shady conditions. You should place your plant outdoors in mid-May. Keep it cool (at 4 to 10 °C/39–50 °F) over the winter. As its name implies, the hydrangea requires a great deal of water. Water it generously with softened, lukewarm water every day from spring through autumn. Water less beginning in August; just keep moist in winter.

Fertilise once per week; discontinue fertiliser after the blooming period; re-pot in spring.

Types

A wide range of shades is available. In "lacecap hydrangeas", inconspicuous single flowers are surrounded by large, striking blossoms.

IMPATIENS WALLERIANA
Impatiens, Busy Lizzy, Balsam

The ever-popular impatiens is a rewarding houseplant whose prototype comes from the tropics of East Africa. Like its close relative, the touch-me-not or Indian balsam, it bears the spurs typical of the balsam family. Its botanical name is derived from the Latin *impatiens* (meaning "sensitive"), due to the fact that its ripe seed capsules will break open at the slightest touch. As the name "busy lizzy" implies, the impatiens blooms abundantly from early spring until late in the autumn, in colours ranging from white through yellow and red to purple; two-toned varieties also exist.

The best location for impatiens is very bright, warm and airy, though somewhat cooler in the winter. It can also be kept outdoors in summer.

Keep the soil consistently moist with softened water; water more sparingly during the rest period. Fertilise lightly once a week during the growth phase. Re-pot only if necessary in spring. Propagate via cuttings: they are easy to root at any time, even in water. You may also propagate via seeds in spring.

Types and Other Species

'Accent Bright Eyes': pale pink with a white eye; 'Starbright': red and white striped; 'Baby': a dwarf variety; 'Mini-Serie': only 15 cm (6 in) tall. *New Guinea* hybrids: the most modern types, tall-growing; longish, coloured leaves; tolerate higher temperatures; easier to keep over the winter. 'Exotica': coloured leaves; 'Tango': flame-red flowers, bronze and green leaves. *Impatiens repens* from Ceylon: yellow flowers with red stems; a creeper, works well as a hanging plant.

IRIS DANFORDIAE
Dwarf iris, Danford iris

This special species of iris, native to Asia Minor and the Caucasus, differs from other irises in that its narrow leaves grow higher than its yellow flowers. The completely winter-hardy dwarf iris needs a sunny location, but should be protected from cold winds. It requires temperatures between 12 °C and 15 °C (54–59 °F) in order to produce flowers.

Water regularly, but never allow the substrate to remain to wet, particularly when there is a danger of frost. Fertiliser is hardly necessary for this plant.
Propagate via division.

> You can easily recognise an attack of botrytis blight by the grey, downy fungus that covers the plant. Avoid excessive moisture if this occurs. Caution is advised when handling the dwarf iris: it contains iridin, a bitter-tasting poison.

IXORA COCCINEA
Flame of the woods, Jungle flame, Jungle geranium

Flame of the woods is an unusually attractive plant which is not very easy to cultivate. This subtly fragrant, usually red-blooming exotic originates in India, and its genus includes more than 200 species. In tropical regions, it often grows as a luxuriantly blooming shrub or as a small tree with pale-orange to orange-red flower umbels.

In our homes, the flame of the woods flourishes best in a winter garden or a warm room. It requires temperatures of at least 20 °C (68 °F) in summer, although it cannot tolerate direct sunlight. Temper-atures should not drop below 15 °C (59 °F) in the winter.
The flame of the woods requires acidic potting soil and relatively high humidity. Under no circumstances should it be placed in an over-sized pot or container, since its root system is not large, and unnecessary spreading of the root ball will quickly tax the plant's strength.
Under proper conditions, the flame of the woods can develop into a sturdy bush, growing 20 to 30 cm (8–12 in) per year.
Water the plant with water that is as soft as possible: boil the water and allow it to stand for one day before using. Propagate via top cuttings (use sections approximately

10–12 cm/4–8 in long). They require temperatures above 22 °C (72 °F) in order to form roots.

JACOBINIA
Jacobinia, Brazilian plume, King's crown, Flamingo flower

The jacobinia, an evergreen member of the acanthus family from Brazil, has given rise to two houseplants which look very different.

J. carnea, the best-known species, takes its name from its flesh- to rose-coloured flowers, which grow together by the bushel on its flower axes. It blooms from June to August. Its leaves are covered with downy hair.

J. pauciflora is more thickly branching, has leathery leaves, and produces many small, individual, nodding red and yellow tube-shaped flowers from December through February.

J. carnea requires a bright to semi-shady location, warm in summer and cooler in winter. It is well-suited to a hothouse or an enclosed plant window, since it requires very moist air. *J. pauciflora*, a plant that is suited to a refrigerated glasshouse, likes a bright to sunny location with moderate humidity. It can spend the summer outdoors; in the winter, it prefers a cool room. Keep the soil moderately moist, depending upon the weather and the rate of growth. Fertilise weekly during the growth period. Prune back in spring and re-pot if necessary.

Propagate *J. carnea* beginning in February, using top cuttings. *J. pauciflora* is propa-

gated in the flowering period, taking top cuttings with thick foliage and without flowers.

JASMINUM
Jasmine

Jasmine, a member of the olive family, originated in the tropics and subtropics. The star-shaped, usually white flowers common to nearly

every species have a wonderful aroma. The petals contain essential oils, and jasmine oil is an ingredient in many perfumes. The jasmine's strong

fragrance can lead to headaches for some people. These delicate climbing shrubs produce long branches which need to be supported in the form of a trellis or arch. Place jasmine in a very bright, airy and moderately warm location; in summer, it enjoys a sheltered outdoor spot. A cool winter rest period is important for the production of new flowers.

Keep the soil moist with softened water in summer; water very sparingly in the winter. Fertilise every two weeks in summer; re-pot in spring if necessary.

Propagate in spring or summer, planting semi-mature cuttings in a propagating case.
Species and Types
J. officinale comes from East Asia and has been cultivated for thousands of years; pleasant fragrance, loses its leaves in autumn; 'Grandiflorum' has very large white flowers. *J. polyanthum*: evergreen, very strong fragrance; flowers are white, tinged with pale pink. *J. mesnyi*: yellow, abundant flowers, relatively frost-resistant. *J. sambac*, Arabian jasmine: originates in India; slow-growing, requires warm temperatures.

KALANCHOE
Kalanchoe

Most of these easy-to-care for members of the stonecrop family come from Madagascar; all have fleshy leaves to some degree. The viviparous species have developed an astonishing method of propagating themselves: tiny plantlets grow along the edges of the leaves, usually developing roots while still attached to the parent plant. They fall off and begin growing immediately when they hit ground. In addition, this genus includes very attractive foliage plants. Flowering varieties need full sun and high temperatures; other types of kalanchoes prefer full sun and moderate temperatures. Viviparous species like dry air; others are content with normal humidity. Water the plants with soft water: keep blooming plants moderately moist, water less in winter. Keep other varieties slightly moist in the summer; in winter, do not water at all if the temperature is low.

Fertilise flowering plants every two to three weeks from March through August; other varieties should receive a little cactus fertiliser in summer. Give the plant a short rest period after the flowering phase, then prune and re-pot if necessary.

Species und Hybriden

Kalanchoe Blossfeldiana hybrids: a group of cultivated

varieties in brilliant colours ranging from yellow to red to violet; the inflorescence lasts for several weeks. *K. manginii*: long, slender, bell-shaped flowers in pink, red or orange; a hanging plant. *K. daigremontiana*, *K. tubiflora* and *K. laxiflora*: viviparous species, formerly called "bryophyllums". *K. pinnata, coirama*, cathedral bells: was a curiosity even in Goethe's time. *K. tomentosa*: silvery, felt-like leaves with rust-coloured hairs along the edges.

LAELIA
Laelia

These attractive orchids inhabit the tropical rainforests from Mexico to Brazil, where they live primarily on trees. The large, richly coloured flowers are located side by side on flower axes; the plants can grow up to a metre tall. Laelias require a bright to semi-shady location with very high humidity: 18 to 24 °C (64–75 °F) in summer, cool in the winter; circulate the air frequently.

Water generously with soft water during the growing period and fertilise lightly with every third watering. Do not water again until the substrate is dry. Do not water too much during the winter rest period, or the plant will shrink.

Re-pot these beauties every two to three years in fresh orchid substrate.

Propagate at the time of repotting by dividing the pseudobulbs.

Species and Hybrids

Laelia purpurata is Brazil's national flower. It is conspicuous for its very large flowers; blooms in spring. *L. cinnabarina*: orange-red flowers, blooms in spring. *L. anceps*: pink-violet; lip is purple, tinged with yellow. *L. pumila*: violet-pink, blooms in autumn; particularly long-lasting. *L. x. harpophylla*: orange flowers, blooms in winter. *L. x. Laeliocattleya*: a hybrid of the laelia and its close relative, cattleya.

LEPTOSPERMUM SCOPARIUM
New Zealand tea tree, Manuka

In Australia and New Zealand, the New Zealand tea tree grows as a tree or shrub; in our homes it is cultivated as a bushy pot plant or a small tall-stemmed tree. Its charming, five-petaled flowers are often pink, but may also be white or carmine red; there are single and compound varieties. The plant's narrow, pointed leaves are fragrant.

The New Zealand tea tree requires a bright, sunny spot. It prefers to be warm in summer, preferably outdoors; put it in a cool room in the winter. Water generously with softened water during the summer; fertilise every two weeks. Keep the soil only moderately moist in winter. Re-pot in spring, if necessary. Prune the plant back occasionally; you may use the cuttings for propagation, if desired.

> The New Zealand tea tree's abundant blossoms almost make its owners forget that this plant requires a great deal of care. However, most indoor gardeners are quite willing to bother with using softened water or water that has stood for several hours—particularly if they have been able to maintain the plant's attractive, bushy shape by pruning after the flowering period.

LITHOPS
Living stones, Flowering stones

These interesting little plants of the fig-marigold family are native to the desert areas of South and Southwest Africa. They are nearly invisible, since they look like gravel stones in their natural environment; this appearance helps to protect the plants from their natural enemies. The living stones consist of two very thick leaves which are conjoined except for a small crevice. In the autumn, an unusually large, yellow or white flower grows from this crevice. The leaves dry out during the rest period; in the following year, a new pair of leaves sprouts up in between them, at right angles to the old pair. The rounded, dome-shaped leaf-tips are often artfully patterned and partly or completely transparent. Some living stones grow below the earth's surface take in light through these "windows".

Living stones like a sunny location at room temperature in summer; in the winter, they prefer to be cool, at 8–10 °C (46–50 °F). Water moderately in the summer (do not water the leaves), and not at all in winter. If necessary, re-pot the plants before the end of the rest period.

Propagate via seeds.

Species

Lithops karasmontana: white flowers, grey and pink leaf patterns. *L. schwantesii var. kuibisensis:* yellow flowers.

117

LOBELIA ERINUS
Lobelia, Edging lobelia

In its South African homeland, the lobelia can often live for several years. In our climate, the delicate plant usually cannot survive the cold winters. Because of its sensitivity to cold, lobelia should not be planted in a window box or outdoor pot before mid-May. There are upright and hanging varieties of lobelias. The first frost means the end of its life, so it has only a short time in which to display its lush array of blue, white and red flowers. The lobelia brings a beautifully coloured accent to its environment, but its care requirements make it a tricky plant. If the weather is cool, it likes to be in the sun; in warm weather it prefers semi-shade.

Water regularly. Should even the tips of its fragile roots become dry, the plant will hold it against you. If its roots are not kept regularly moist, the lobelia will die very quickly.

Begin fertilising four weeks after re-potting. After that, supplement every week with a fertiliser that contains potassium.

Propagate via seeds.

Types

'Alba' is white; 'Pendula Sapphire' has dark blue flowers with white centres.

MAMMILLARIA
Mammillaria, Feather cactus, Pincushion cactus

One of our most popular cacti is the mammillaria, whose natural habitat stretches from Mexico to Colombia. You can recognise it by the fact that its ribs dissolve into the characteristic round or angled nipples, whose arrangement is extremely variable. The shape and size of the mammillaria's thorn patterns also varies widely. Just below the top of the cactus, a thick crown of small white, yellow, pink or red flowers forms. Mammillarias sprout up strongly and form cushions; some varieties tend to grow in a comb shape. Young plants often develop in a ring around the base of the parent cactus.

The mammillaria is most at home in a refrigerated glasshouse. It likes an airy, bright and warm location in summer: the densely thorned varieties prefer sunnier homes than the green, naked types. In winter, place the cactus in a cool, bright, airy and dry room. Water from below with soft, warm water in summer; keep dry in winter. Re-pot in cactus substrate after the blooming period, if necessary. Propagate via offshoots or seeds.

Species and Types

Mammillaria zeilmanniana, the most attractive species, has dense white thorns and fine hairs; dark pink flowers appear in the summer. *M. bocasana*: fast-growing; thorns are curved into a hook shape. *M. plumosa*, feather cactus: delicate thorns; blooms in winter and should therefore be kept warmer in winter. *M. vaupelii* 'Cristata': comb shape, made up of many thorn-covered "sausages". *M. wildii*: very attractive thorn pattern; fast-growing. *M. prolifera*: indestructible.

MARANTA LEUCONEURA
Prayer plant, Rabbit's tracks

This striking member of the family Marantaceae—named after the Italian doctor and herbalist Bartolomeo Maranta—comes from the American tropics. Its ornately patterned leaves have a typical sleeping position: when darkness falls, they roll themselves up like bags standing on end. The prayer plant is capable of producing flowers, but its small white blossoms are quite inconspicuous. In the past, it was only possible to grow prayer plants in hothouses: today, they can be seen in enclosed plant windows as well as in rooms. Hydroponic culture is also possible.

The prayer plant requires a bright location which must be warm throughout the year. High humidity and consistently moist soil are musts.

Water generously with pleasantly warm, softened water; mist frequently. Fertilise every two weeks in summer; repot in spring if necessary.

Propagate in spring via division.

Species and Types

'Kerchoveana': emerald green leaves with ten large, velvety brown spots. 'Massangeana': leaf undersides are dark red. 'Erythroneura': emerald green leaves with red side veins. 'Fascinator': inner sections of leaves are yellow-green, outer sections dark green with red side veins. *Maranta bicolour*: velvety brown spots on both sides of the centre vein; lighter middle stripes; leaf undersides are red-violet. *M. arundinacea*: a food plant in the tropics, its tuber-like roots contain valuable starches.

MEDINILLA MAGNIFICA
Medinilla, Malaysian orchid, Rose grape

One of the most impressive flowering plants is the magnificent medinilla, a melastome native to the Philippines. From early spring

through August, the medinilla produces countless rose-coloured flowers clustered together in overhanging flower axes up to 40 cm (15 in) long and topped with pale-pink bracts. The dark green leaves are thick and leathery and can grow be 30 cm (12 in) long; the branches are four-sided. The medinilla grows up to 1 to 1.5 metres (3–5 ft) in the rainforest; it requires plenty of space in the home as well. It is a very demanding hothouse plant: it flourishes well in an enclosed plant window. Its location needs to be bright, but without direct sunlight, and very humid. The plant should be kept warm in summer, somewhat cooler during its rest period, from November to February.

> The medinilla is only slightly susceptible to pests; however, it is a very demanding plant. As an exotic beauty from the Philippines, it is very unhappy when the humidity is too low, and may react with stunted growth.

Keep the soil uniformly moist with warm, soft water; mist frequently. Water more sparingly during the rest period. Fertilise weekly from March through August. Re-pot in the early spring if necessary.

119

MICROCOELUM WEDDELIANUM
Miniature coconut palm, Wedding palm

This delicate little palm, with its graceful, feathery leaves, originates in the Brazilian rainforests. It grows to a maximum height of 1.5 metres (5 ft); its feathery leaves are arranged in even rows. Unfortunately, the wedding palm does not last long in our homes, since it is rarely provided with the conditions it needs to survive. It feels most at home in an enclosed plant window or a winter garden.

Place the wedding palm in a bright, very humid location, away from the full sun. The temperature should be at least 20 °C (68 °F). Keep the soil moist at all times with soft, warm water; mist frequently. The wedding palm loves extended footbaths: it needs to have water in its saucer. Re-pot only when necessary (every two to three years), taking care not to damage the roots. Lay plenty of clay pot shards over the drainage holes in the bottom of the pot.

Propagation is difficult: via seeds at a soil temperature of 30 °C.

> The miniature coconut palm does not like to be moved. Thus, you should only re-pot it as often as necessary. Be careful: if you damage the plant's roots in the process, it may die very quickly.

MONSTERA
Split-leaf philodendron

The split-leaf philodendron, a native of the Mexican tropics, is a member of the arum lily family. Its name comes from the Latin *monstrum*—probably a reference to its large, oddly formed leaves. Young leaves are heart-shaped; they later develop holes ("windows") and deep grooves. They are shiny, leathery and evergreen, and can grow up to 60 cm (24 in) long.

This plant grows rapidly and requires plenty of space. Well-cared for, its lifespan can equal that of a person! Older plants develop many aerial roots. As soon as these touch the ground, they become normal roots and take in nutrients. Only older plants produce flowers and fruit. *Monstera* is comfortable at room temperature. It likes bright as well as shady conditions: it should definitely not be placed in the sun. The brighter its spot, the larger the leaves will grow. As a native of the tropics, it loves humidity; since it is a climbing shrub, it requires support. Keep the root ball moist, water with pleasantly warm water, more in summer than in winter. Fertilise every week in summer; re-pot once per year. Carefully guide any aerial roots (they are fragile) into moist soil or a container of water; do not cut them off. Wipe the leaves off occasionally with a damp cloth; mist frequently with lukewarm water.

Propagation: plant cuttings containing aerial roots in the soil, or root in water. Mossing is also possible.

Species and Types

Monstera deliciosa 'Variegata' is noteworthy for its irregular, creamy white patterns.

'Borsigiana' is a smaller variety. *M. obliqua* can be recognised by its elongated holes.

MYRTUS COMMUNIS
Myrtle, True Myrtle, Roman Myrtle

This pretty little shrub, whose family also bears its name, can be found growing wild in the Mediterranean region. The myrtle was sacred to the goddess Aphrodite, and was considered a symbol of fertility. Later, it was worn by brides as a symbol of purity. Myrtle blooms in midsummer, producing many delightful, fragrant white flowers, all with numerous long stamens. Even the leathery, evergreen leaves give off an aromatic scent when rubbed together. Like the plant's blackish-violet berries, they contain essential oils.

The myrtle has always been recognised as a healing plant.

Even today, its leaves and berries are used to make liqueurs. The myrtle likes a bright, sunny, airy location that is warm in summer; you can also place it outdoors. In winter, keep it at temperatures of 5 to 8 °C (41–46 °F). Keep the soil evenly moist with soft, room temperature water; water less in winter. Avoid standing water; but do not let the root ball dry out. Supplement each week in summer with lime-free fertiliser. Repot in spring only if necessary. You can cut your myrtle into a desired shape, but it will not bloom if you do this. Propagate via cuttings.

NARCISSUS
Narcissus, Daffodil

This pretty member of the amaryllis family is known primarily as a garden plant. However, you can also grow nearly every variety in pots or dishes. Most types first require a rooting period in a cool, dark place. In the autumn, place the bulbs in a flat dish filled with gravel, twice as deep as the bulbs' diameter. Only move them back into the light when you can clearly feel the flower buds pushing out of the bulbs. Keep the soil moderately moist at all times. The golden yellow 'Grand Soleil d'Or' and the white-blossomed Christmas narcissus 'Paper White' can be placed in a light location from the very beginning.

After the flowering period, continue to water the plants until their leaves turn yellow. Then, reduce the amount of water and allow the plant to dry out somewhat.

Store the bulbs in a cool place in summer—e.g., in the cellar. Wait until autumn to re-plant them.

By planting your bulbs at two-week intervals, you can significantly extend the period in which you can enjoy blooming narcissus.

NEOREGELIA

Neoregelia, Bloody bromeliad

This tropical, Brazilian member of the pineapple family has long leaves edged with thorny teeth. They form a rosette whose innermost leaves take on striking colours during the blooming period and maintain them for months. The neoregelia's leaves may be green, shiny, striped or

speckled; the central rosettes are usually red, but may be purple or yellow. The tiny flowers sit inside the funnel as if in a nest. Like all bromeliads, each of the leaf funnels blooms only once. This plant looks very decorative on an epiphyte stalk or in a warm, humid plant window.

The location should be very bright, but not exposed to the blazing sun. Cultivate young plants in a hothouse; older plants will also tolerate room conditions.

Keep this plant warm; in winter, at 18 °C (64 °F). A blooming plant will last longer if placed in a cooler location. Fill the leaf rosette with soft, warm water; keep the root ball uniformly moist. Change the water in the funnel every two weeks, and fertilise lightly. Keep the air very moist in summer, less so in winter.

Propagation via offshoots: separate them as soon as they develop roots. Seed propagation is possible, but will result in green-leaved plants.

Species and Types

Neoreglia carolinae: red centre leaves; 'Tricolor' has creamy white, striped leaves. *N. concentrica*: purple centre leaves, speckled outer leaves.

NEPHROLEPIS EXALTATA

Boston fern, Sword fern

This very attractive tropical fern can grow either on the ground or as an epiphyte. Its scientific name comes from the Greek *nephros* ("kidney") and *lepis* ("scale"). Its light green, feathery fronds grow relatively fast and can reach lengths of up to 70 cm (27 in). They hang over gracefully, making the Boston fern an ideal hanging plant.

Its location should be bright to semi-shady and warm; however, temperatures should not exceed 18 °C (64 °F) in the winter and do avoid drafts. High humidity is extremely important.

Keep your Boston fern consistently moist with soft water, and mist frequently; supplement regularly with weak doses of fertiliser. Re-pot every spring.

Propagation usually takes place in summer, via runners or division; pure species may be propagated via spores.

Species and Types

Nephrolepis exaltata: e.g. 'Maassii', with multiply feathered fronds; 'Rooseveltii' has wavy feathers; 'Teddy Junior' with wavy and twisted feathers. *N. cordifolia* 'Plumosa' is more delicate; double feathers.

NERIUM OLEANDER
Oleander

These magnificently blooming shrubs, native to the Mediterranean region, are members of the dogbane family. They grow along riverbanks, where soil is sometimes dry on the surface but moist below ground. Oleander can be up to 5 metres (16 ft) tall.

The oleander has leathery, lancet-like, evergreen leaves and rose-coloured single flowers. Types with white, yellow, purple and compound flowers also exist; however, these cultivated varieties do not display the same lush growth.

Oleander requires a sunny, hot location with plenty of fresh air: in other words, you should place it outdoors from spring through autumn. It can also survive light night-time frosts over short periods.

Keep the plant in a bright and cool location in winter, at temperatures between 5 °C and 10 °C (41–50 °F).

Water generously in summer; the plant enjoys footbaths. Fertilise once per week; water less in the winter. Re-pot in spring if necessary.

Propagate in the summer by rooting cuttings in water. Be sure to wear gloves to prune your oleander, since all parts of the plant are poisonous.

NERTERA GRANADENSIS
Coral bead plant, pincushion plant

This charming member of the coffee family, a native of the Andes, takes its name from the Greek word *nerteros* (low), since it grows only a few centimetres tall and can creep across the ground. This delightful little plant blooms in April, producing tiny, inconspicuous, greenish-white flowers. In August, it produces large quantities of tiny, barely pea-sized, gleaming orange-red berries. They cover the light green leaves almost entirely and last until the winter. The coral bead plant is happiest in a cool, bright location with plenty of fresh air; tem-

peratures of 10 to 12 °C (50–54 °F) are sufficient in winter. Keep the soil evenly moist in summer; water sparingly from autumn to spring. It is best to water from below.

Fertilise lightly every four weeks from March through August. If you fertilise too heavily, the leaves will obscure the decorative berries. Re-pot in shallow containers in spring. Propagate via division once the fruits fall off.

It is best to propagate your coral bead plant in August or September. Use a sharp knife to divide the plant. The new plant will feel most at home in soil that is sandy, humus and contains some clay.

NOTOCACTUS
Ball cactus, Golden ball

These pretty, rewarding cacti from South America have numerous, diagonally divided ribs and widely varying, often conspicuous thorns. The large, usually yellow flowers arise from near the top of the plant, even in quite young specimens. The ball cactus prefers a bright location in spring and summer, out of the blazing sun. In summer you can keep it indoors or let it stand outside. In winter, it should live in a cool, dry room where the temperature does not go below 10 °C (50 °F).

Keep the soil consistently moist in summer, using water that has been allowed to stand; keep dry in winter. In summer, fertilise lightly every two weeks with low-nitrogen cactus fertiliser; re-pot in cactus substrate as necessary. Propagate via seeds.

Species

Notocactus apricus: small. *N. cocinnus*: yellow or reddish thorns. *N. leninghausii*, golden ball cactus: silky yellow flowers, thick golden-yellow thorns; the top of the cactus turns toward the light. *N. ottonis*: yellow to brown thorns. *N. scopa*: fuzzy white. *N. uebelmannianus*: balls can grow up to 17 cm (6 in) in diameter; flowers are yellow to dark red.

OPUNTIA
Prickly pear, Opuntia

The original home of these unusual cacti is an area ranging from Canada to Patagonia. Many species have been carried to other parts of the world and can now be found even in the Mediterranean region. Prickly pear cacti may have disk-shaped, flattened stems or cylindrical limbs. Their large, shimmering flowers are brilliantly coloured.

A characteristic feature of the prickly pear is its glochidia — tiny, barbed bristles which break off when touched and remain under the skin. They are also on the cactus fruit, so be sure to wear gloves!

In summer, place your prickly pear in a sunny, warm, airy location, preferably outdoors. In winter, put it in a bright, cool room; winter-hardy species can remain out-of-doors. Keep the soil moderately moist when the ground is dry in summer; supplement with a little cactus fertiliser. Depending on the temperature in winter, keep the soil nearly or completely dry. Re-pot approximately every two years in the early spring.

Propagate via cuttings: allow the cut-off edge to dry for two weeks before planting. Seed propagation is also possible.

Species

Opuntia microdasys, bunny ears or polka dot cactus: yellow flowers, many cultivated varieties, e.g. *var. albispina*, white bunny ears. *O. bergeriana*: blooms abundantly, tile-coloured red flowers. *O. fiscus-indica*, Indian fig: yellow flowers, very tasty fruit; cultivated in warm countries, grows rapidly.

OXALIS
Wood sorrel, Shamrock

The name oxalis is derived from the Greek *oxys* (sour) and *halos* (salt). The wood sorrel family is also called the sour grass family. This plant is frequently sold around New Year's Day. The shamrock or "four-leafed clover" is no relation to true clover, even though its stems of three to four leaves look quite similar. The leaves fold together in a sleeping position each evening. The wood sorrel's location should be cool all year round, and as bright as possible. You can place the little plant outdoors from May until autumn. Bring the bulbs inside before the first frost and store them in a cool, dry place. The plant normally takes a rest period until spring. The blooming plants we see in shops for the New Year have been raised from pre-cooled bulbs.

Water sparingly during cultivation; somewhat more if temperatures are high. Fertilise once a week during the growth period.

Propagate via bulblets.

Species and Types

Oxalis deppei is a Mexican strain with four-leaf clusters; flowers are dark pink; 'Braunherz' has leaves that are dark brown at the base. *O. adenophylla*: greyish-green, three-leaf clusters, pink flowers.

PACHYPODIUM
Madagascar palm, Club foot, Elephant's trunk

This strange-looking member of the dogbane family from tropical Madagascar looks like a combination of a cactus and a palm tree. Its thick, columnar trunk, which is studded with sharp thorns, gives rise to a rosette of long, narrow leaves. Where an old leaf falls off, three thorns remain.

In the wild this palm grows to a 6 to 10 metre (20–33 ft) tree. In our homes, it will reach 1 metre (3 ft) after ten years. White, star-shaped flowers may appear when the plant is about 1.2 metres (4 ft) tall. The trunk and leaves of the Madagascar palm contain a highly poisonous sap; the thorns can also inflict injury.

The Madagascar palm likes a bright, sunny and warm location throughout the year. Unlike most other plants, its growth period takes place during the winter, with a rest period in summer. It will even tolerate dry, centrally-heated air.

Keep the soil moderately moist in winter, dry in the summer. Fertilise very lightly during the winter. The plant likes warm soil temperatures; avoid standing water; re-pot infrequently.

Propagate via seeds.

Species

Pachypodium lamerei: wide, light green leaves, best-known species; *P. geayi*: its long, narrow, silver-grey leaves are reddish on the underside.

> The Madagascar palm takes its name from its homeland. The most luxuriant species, the dwarf pachypodium, only finds ideal conditions there and often doesn't survive as a houseplant. This was not known until after an import ban was imposed, which prevented the digging up and exporting of older plants.

PACHYSTACHYS LUTEA
Golden shrimp plant, Lollipop plant, Golden candle

Like the shrimp plant or false hop, the golden shrimp plant, a native of Peru, is a member of the acanthus family. It was extremely popular over a century ago and was then forgotten. Now it is once again being sold as a new product. The golden shrimp plant bears attractive, upright, gleaming yellow flower heads made up of long-lasting spathes. The actual flowers peek out from in between the spathes: they are white and wither quickly.

The best location for this plant is warm and bright to very bright; it likes high humidity. Temperatures should not go below 18 °C (64 °F) in winter. Water the plant moderately during the growth phase, less in the winter. Once the first shoots appear in spring, fertilise once per week. Re-pot in spring, pruning beforehand if necessary.

Propagate in spring using top cuttings from non-flowering branches; root the cuttings in a propagating case; support young plants at several points.

> This plant with its highly descriptive names may fail to produce flowers. However, with diligent care, you can prevent a worst-case scenario. The plant will only refuse to bloom if it lacks light, warmth or fertiliser.

PANDANUS
Screw pine, Pandanus, Pandan

A native of the tropics, the screw pine has lent its name to its entire family of plants. It grows rapidly, and quickly requires a great deal of space for its wide, spiny tuft of leaves. The screw pine's name refers to its leaves, which grow in a spiral pattern out of the plant's short trunk. They are overhanging, and can grow 1 to 2 metres (3–6 ft) long. Within a few years, the screw pine develops a large number of strong, woody aerial roots which take over the support function of the trunk and lift the plant out over the sides of its pot—a completely natural occurrence. The screw pine also develops offshoots.

This plant requires a bright location, high humidity and warm conditions throughout the year. Keep the soil moist with warm water at all times during the summer; water less in winter. Fertilise weekly from March through August.

Re-pot young plants every year, older ones less often. Do not set the plant too deeply in the soil.

Propagate with offshoots that are 20 cm (8 in) long.

Species

Pandanus veitchii: originally from Polynesia, with long, narrow, white and green striped leaves edged with thick thorns. *P. sanderi:* from the Malaysian archipelago; leaves have yellow stripes and fine thorns along the edges. *P. utilis* comes from Madagascar, where it grows to 20 metres (65 ft) tall; robust, blue-green leaves with red, thorny edges.

PAPHIOPEDILUM
Lady's slipper orchid, Paphiopedilum

This orchid's evergreen leaves are mottled green, speckled or marbled; its flowers radiate in every shade of white, yellow, green, brown and purple and may be striped, speckled or piebald. The plant itself grows on the surface of the earth.

The lady's slipper orchid does not produce pseudobulbs; each leaf rosette blooms only once. New rosettes form which bloom in the following year.

The lady's slipper orchid requires a very humid location, removed from direct sunlight in summer and bright in the winter. The green-leaved plants prefer room temperature in the daytime; at night and in winter, they like to be cooler. The marbled-leaf varieties are

hothouse plants: they should be kept at temperatures of at least 18 °C (64 °F), even in winter. Water moderately with soft, room temperature water, only when the soil has dried out. Water sparingly in winter. Supplement with low doses of fertiliser every three weeks from April through September. Mist the leaves on sunny days; re-pot if necessary after the blooming period.

Propagate via division when re-potting.

Species

Paphiopedilum callosum, has blue-green leaves, originally from Thailand. *P. fairrieanum*: from Sikkim. *P. sukhakulii*: mottled leaves. *P. hirsutissimum*.

PARODIA
Parodia

These charming little ball-shaped cacti come from South America. They grow slowly, to a maximum height of 20 cm (8 in). The ribs are often arranged in a spiral and dissolve into warts or knobs, from which large, attractive thorns grow. Even young plants can produce gorgeous flowers in every shade of yellow and red from their woolly crowns.

In summer, the parodia likes a bright, sunny and airy location; in the winter, it should be kept cool and dry.

Keep the soil slightly moist in summer; supplement with a little cactus fertiliser every two to three weeks. Water from below; in winter, do not water at all. If necessary, re-pot every two years in spring. Propagate via seeds.

Species

Parodia mairanana: brilliant red flowers. *P. mutabifis*: light to golden yellow and yellow-orange flowers. *P. nivosa*: snow-white thorns, flame red flowers. *P. maassii*: light green with stiff thorns and copper-coloured flowers. *P. sanguiniflora*: blood-red flowers. *P. chrysacanthion*: yellow flowers. *P. aureispina*: flowers and thorns are golden yellow.

PASSIFLORA

Passion flower, Granadilla, Maracuja

The tropical American passion flower has lent its name to its entire family of plants. Its own name was bestowed by a Jesuit priest from Peru, who interpreted the individual parts of these unusual flowers as symbols for the suffering of Christ. The fast-growing climbing shrubs, with branches that can grow several metres long, will happily spiral up-

wards on trellises or frames. Sometimes the plants will also develop fruits.

The passion flower needs a bright, sunny and airy location which should be warm in the summer: some species even prefer a sheltered place outdoors. A cool rest period in the winter—at 7 to 10 °C (45–50 °F), depending upon the species—will encourage renewed flower production. Water the plant generously in summer and fertilise once per week; water only sparingly in winter. Prune back in spring; re-pot young plants every year, older ones less often.

Propagate with cuttings planted at soil temperatures of 22 °C (72 °F); you can propagate older plants via root offshoots.

Species and Types

Passiflora caerulea, blue passion flower, is the most common species and has whitish flowers with blue crosshairs; 'Kaiserin Eugenie' is reddish, 'Constance Illiot' is cream-coloured. *P. incarnata*: white to pale reddish flowers with a wreath of purple rays in the centre, is very robust. Heat-loving species include *P. quadrangularis*, the quick-growing giant granadilla with very large, multi-coloured fragrant blossoms, and *P. racemosa*, which has scarlet flowers.

PELARGONIUM

Scented pelargonium and geranium, Pelargonium

Pelargoniums originate in South Africa. Scented pelargoniums generally have feathered leaves which emit an intense aroma; in contrast to geraniums, their flowers are relatively inconspicuous. The popular varieties frequently used as patio or window box plants are known as "geraniums". Their flowers appear in many brilliant colours; the leaves have serrated edges. Hanging and upright varieties are available. Pelargoniums like an airy and very bright location. They prefer to be warm in summer and cooler in winter. Fertilise every two weeks in summer; dead-head regularly. Prune the plants and re-pot in spring or autumn. Propagate with the cuttings taken during pruning.

Species and Types
Scented Pelargoniums
Pelargonium graveolens: a wonderfully aromatic wild variety with small, pink to purple-red flowers and lobed, hand-shaped leaves. *P. radens* also has a rose-like fragrance. *P. x. citrosmum* (*syn. crispum*) and *P. odoratissimum* have a lemony scent; 'Prince of Orange' and 'Scarlet Pet' smell like oranges. *P. capitatum* is a source of geranium oil. *P. tomentosum* has a peppermint scent; *P. quercifolium* smells like camphor. *P. fragrans* has a piney-citrus aroma; 'Els' has a strong flowery scent.

Geraniums
Grandiflorum hybrids (regal pelargoniums): a natural flowering period for these plants is actually summer, but they can be purchased in bloom all year round. Varieties include 'Aquarell', 'Autumn Festival', 'Purple Emperor' and 'Valentin'. Good plants for the patio are the *Zonale* hybrids (horseshoe geraniums) and *Peltatum* hybrids (ivy geraniums).

PELLAEA ROTUNDIFOLIA
Button fern, Roundleaf fern

In its homeland of New Zealand this unique, atypical fern can be found in dry, sunny locations on limestone cliffs. Its name comes from the Greek *pellos* (blackish), a reference to its leaves. Its delicate, 20 to 30 cm (8–12 in) long fronds consist of little rounded, dark green leaves which have a leathery shine. Its overhanging or creeping fronds make the button fern an excellent choice as a hanging plant or a ground cover.

Button fern prefers an airy and semi-shady spot. It likes room temperature in summer, somewhat cooler temperatures in winter (ca. 15 °C/59 °F). Water normally in summer with room temperature water, somewhat less in the winter; it is sensitive to excessive moisture. Fertilise lightly throughout the summer; re-pot in shallow dishes in spring if necessary. Propagate via division or spores.

Other Species

Pellaea viridis: comes from South Africa and Madagascar; upright and bushy; green fronds up to 75 cm (29 in) long. *P. falcata* is native to South Asia, Australia and New Zealand. *P. atropurpurea*: native of North America; a lime-loving, nearly winter hardy cliff or rock-dwelling

fern with dark, purplish-red fronds up to 25 cm (10 in).

PENTAS IANCEOLATA
Pentas, Star cluster, Star flower

This charming member of the coffee family originated in the Middle East, tropical Africa and Madagascar. It is a popular garden plant in tropical countries. Its name comes from the Greek *pente* (five), a reference to its five-pointed blossoms. The star-shaped flowers grow in inflorescences of 10 to 30 long-necked individual blossoms. They come in every shade of pink, white and red; the light green, oval leaves are relatively large and hairy.

Pentas require a bright spot out of the blazing sun, and very high humidity. Place it in a warm airy location — even outdoors — in summer; keep it cool in winter, between 10 and 15 °C (50–59 °F).

Water moderately with soft, warm water during the growth period; avoid standing water. Keep the soil drier once the flowering is past. Fertilise lightly every two weeks in summer; re-pot in spring.

Propagate using leafy top cuttings, planted at soil temperatures of 20 to 25 °C (68–77 °F).

Standing water, cold feet and hard water are all horrors for the pentas. Yellow leaves will be the result. However, if you follow the care instructions closely, and also prune the plant back frequently, it will bloom abundantly in your indoor garden.

PEPEROMIA
Peperomia, Baby rubber plant

These pretty little members of the pepper family have their native home in the tropical and subtropical forests of America. Most of them are epiphytic—that is, they sit on the branches of other plants. They are cultivated primarily as foliage plants, since most of their leaves have interesting colours, patterns, shapes and structures. Only a few varieties develop their characteristic, worm-shaped flower axes in cultivation. Peperomias have the ability to store water inside their thick leaves and branches. These charming little plants are ideally suited to epiphyte stalks or plant windows.

Green varieties prefer bright to semi-shady conditions; coloured types like it very bright, but not sunny. Plants with fleshy leaves tolerate dry indoor air; the soft-leaved species require higher humidity. All types like to be fairly warm throughout the year.

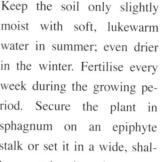

Keep the soil only slightly moist with soft, lukewarm water in summer; even drier in the winter. Fertilise every week during the growing period. Secure the plant in sphagnum on an epiphyte stalk or set it in a wide, shallow container in spring.

Propagate in spring via cuttings.

Species and Types

Peperomia caperata, emerald ripple peperomia: the leaves are deeply furrowed; white flower heads reach upward to the sky. *P. otusifolia*: has shiny, stiff leaves, marbled white or yellow; 'Greengold' has more distinct leaf patterns; 'Minima' is a dwarf variety. *P. griseoargentea*: has grey-green leaves which are very wavy between the veins; *P. serpens* (*scandens*): branches are initially creeping, later also upright; 'Variegata' is a coloured-leaf variety. *P. fraseri* has a captivating aroma.

PETUNIA X HYBRIDA CULTIVAR
Garden petunia

Countless hybrids have been cultivated from the petunia, which originally comes from South America. Its spectrum of colours ranges from white through every shade of red and pink to beautiful blue and violet tones. There is equal variety in flower shape: they may be large or small, single or compound, smooth or curly. Petunias make the most attractive impression anywhere that their branches can hang down as freely as possible. As soon as any threat of frost is over, you can place your petunias outdoors: they are happiest in full sunshine. On days when the sun does not shine, the flowers will remain closed. Petunias are very sensitive to rain. An incredible abundance of blossoms that lasts into the late autumn is a characteristic trait of the petunia. Begin fertilising at weekly intervals one month after planting.

Propagate via seeds.

Types

'Pendula' varieties are particularly well suited to patio baskets or hanging pots: their overhanging tendrils grow up to 80 cm (30 in) long; 'Surfina' is a very attractive variety. 'Multiflora' types grow upright and compact. Yet smaller are the 'Nana' and 'Nana compacta' types.

Petunias are susceptible to attacks of nicotiana viruses, which may be spread via hands or equipment, or by insects. For this reason, it is important to combat pests as early as possible, keep your equipment clean and destroy any affected plants.

PHALAENOPSIS
Moth orchid

The lovely moth orchid originates in the humid rainforests between India and northern Australia, where it grows on the tops of trees. Some species really do resemble moths or butterflies. They do not produce pseudobulbs, but have many roots. Their tongue-shaped leaves are dark green, the spectacular flowers may be white, yellow, pink, red, violet, brown or green. They are found in a variety of shapes and patterns and are very long-lasting.

The moth orchid is a hot-house plant: it requires very high humidity and room temperature or warmer. Only in autumn should you keep it at 12 to 16 °C (54–61 °F) for a few weeks. Place the orchid in a shady spot in summer; bright, but never sunny in the winter. Keep the soil moderately moist with soft water; water even less during the rest period. Allow the substrate to dry out in between waterings, but never let the plant dry out completely. Do not water the plant at its centre, since there is a danger of rotting; mist frequently. Supplement with orchid fertiliser every two weeks in the summer; re-pot every two to three years in spring.

Occasional propagation via offshoots is possible.

Species and Hybrids

Phalaenopsis amabilis: is the prototype species, and its flowers may be white, pink or purple. Hybrids are easier to care for than the pure species, especially appropriate for beginners. A large variety of colours is available—for example, 'Mambo': green-gold with pink lips; 'Cassandra': white with purplish-red lips; 'Hokuspokus' has speckled flowers. Multi-species hybrids also exist.

PHILODENDRON
Philodendron

The philodendron, a native of the American tropics, is a member of the arum lily family. As its name implies—Greek *philein* means "to love" and *dendron* "tree"—most species like to climb up the sides of trees; many produce aerial roots. There are tree-like and shrub-like species with complete, lobed or segmented leaves, which are evergreen, shiny, and highly decorative. If you are lucky, an older plant may even produce a flower similar to that of the arum lily.

Place your philodendron in a bright to shady location, away from direct sunlight. It greatly appreciates high humidity. Air, water and soil should all be maintained at room temperature.

From spring through August, keep the soil uniformly moist with soft water; water more sparingly in the autumn and winter; mist frequently. Supplement with a low-lime fertiliser every two weeks from April to August; re-pot the plant once per year, older plants less often.

Propagate using runners bearing aerial roots, top or axil cuttings, seeds or even mossing.

Species and Types

Philodendron scandens: the best-known species; unassuming; tolerates shade; small, heart-shaped leaves; good as a hanging plant or a green cover for walls or trellises. *P. erubescens*: has long, arrow-shaped leaves; flowers have cinnamon-coloured spathes and creamy white spadices; 'Red Emerald' and 'Bourgogne' varieties have somewhat reddish leaves; attractive for plant windows. 'Lynette', the newest variety, has atypical, tongue-shaped leaves. *P. selloum*: non-climbing; leaf edges are notched and wavy.

131

PHOENIX
Phoenix palm, Dwarf date palm

The ancient Greeks already knew the date palm by the name *Phoenix*. It is a robust house or patio plant and can reach heights of 1 to 2 metres (3–7 ft) inside the home. The phoenix palm has feathered, slightly overhanging leaves.

Its location should be warm and very bright; Canary Island and true date palms tolerate full sun; they may go outdoors in the summer. The phoenix palm likes room temperature: even in winter, temperatures should not fall below 16 °C (61 °F). The Canary Island and true date palms will tolerate somewhat cooler conditions.

Keep soil moist with warm, soft water; less in winter. Mist frequently to increase humidity. Fertilise lightly in summer; re-pot only when needed. Propagate via seeds.

Species
Phoenix dactylifera, true date palm of North Africa; bears edible fruit; brownish-green leaves. These palms can be cultivated from date seeds; fast-growing. *P. canariensis,* Canary Island date palm: brilliant green leaves, short trunk. *P. roebelenii,* dwarf date palm from Southeast Asia: soft, narrow, delicately overhanging leaves; demanding species; requires warmer conditions.

PHYLLITIS SCOLOPENDRIUM
Hart's tongue fern

The hart's tongue fern is a tongue-shaped fern of the spleenwort family. Its non-feathered, fully-edged fronds are a smooth, shiny green and

can grow up to 40 cm (15 in) long. Fringed, grooved and curly varieties are also available. *Scolopendrium* means "centipede-like", and refers to the arrangement of the fern's lineal spore deposits, located on the underside of the fronds. The hart's tongue fern grows in moist, shady, limestone regions, even in Europe. Its ideal location is shady to semi-shady, airy, moist and cool. It likes summer temperatures of 15 to 18 °C (59–64 °F) and may be placed outdoors. In winter, keep it at around 10 °C (50 °F); the plant requires consistent moisture. Water moderately; fertilise lightly every two weeks during the growing period; mist frequently.

Propagate species via spores; varieties via division or by rooting the ends of leaf stems which contain a section of rhizome in warm soil.

Types
'Cristata', 'Crispa', 'Undulata': long, wavy fronds. 'Capitata' is curly at the tips. 'Ramosa Marginata' and 'Ramosa Cristata' have parsley-like leaves. 'Digitata', fingered hart's tongue; 'Inequale Varians' has antler-like branches.

A typical fern, the hart's tongue will react immediately to over-dry air. Since it is actually an outdoor plant, it doesn't like to be too warm. In both cases, the fronds will dry out and the plant will be vulnerable to thrips attacks.

PILEA
Aluminium plant, Artillery plant

One interesting member of the nettle family is the aluminium or artillery plant. Its name comes from the fact that, as soon as the flowers come in contact with water, their filaments draw themselves together and "shoot" clouds of pollen out into their environment. These low-growing plants, with their attractively patterned leaves, are well suited as ground covers for plant windows or dish plantings.

Place the aluminium plant in a bright to semi-shady, warm location with a high relative humidity; the location should be somewhat cooler in winter. Keep the soil uniformly moist in summer with soft, pleasantly warm water. Water somewhat less in the winter. Fertilise every one or two weeks during the growth period; do not mist the leaves. Prune and re-pot the aluminium plant in spring.

Propagate using cuttings taken during pruning.

Species and Types

Pilea cadierei, aluminium plant: green, slightly thrown-open leaves with silvery patterns. *P. crassifolia* 'Moon Valley': wrinkly, light green leaves with blackish-brown veins. *P. spruceana*: bronze-green leaves with silvery stripes. *P. nummulariifolia*: a small-leaved hanging plant.

PLATYCERIUM
Staghorn fern, Elkhorn fern, Platycerium, Elephant ear fern

The staghorn fern is an unusual-looking fern: its branching fronds, which can often grow several metres long, resemble the antlers of a deer or elk. It lives epiphytically in the forks of tropical rainforest trees, where decomposed parts of plants often collect.

The staghorn fern has two types of leaves: infertile alcoves or bracts anchor the plant. As soon as they turn brown and begin to rot, they are converted to humus and supply the plant with nutrients. The fertile spore leaves bear flat, black-brown spore pods on their mostly branching fronds. In their younger stage, these leaves are often covered with white down (do not wipe it off!). Keep your staghorn fern in a hanging pot or on an epiphyte stalk.

This fern loves a semi-shady location at room temperature; at night and in winter, the temperature may sink as low as 14 °C (57 °F). Water the plant into its bracts with soft, room temperature water; or you can immerse the plant for 30 minutes once a week. Add a little fertiliser to the water from April through August. Keep the humidity high; do not wipe off the fronds and do not mist this plant.

Species

Platycerium bifurcatum, from Australian tropics, is the best-known species; sterile fronds are slightly grooved; fertile ones are pale grey-green and forked in two or three places. *P. grande*: from Luzon; sterile fronds are light green and slightly wavy, notched at the ends; spore leaves grow more than a metre long with a distinctly branching, antler-like shape; fertile leaves have fluffy hairs when young. *P. angolense*: from Africa; non-segmented spore leaves.

PORTULACA GRANDIFLORA
Moss rose, Portulaca

The moss rose, a native of Brazil, is a true sun-worshipper. If you place it in direct sunlight, sheltered from rain, it will reward you with an incredible abundance of flowers from summer into early autumn. Keep the plant protected from rain and wind. The low-growing moss rose can be found in single and compound-flower varieties, in a wide range of colours from white to red to pink to yellow. Its flowers, which can grow to 8 cm (3 in) tall, will only open when the sun shines.

The moss rose is not winter hardy. It is fairly forgiving of watering errors, since its thick leaves can store water for a long time. However, regular watering will ensure you a delightful crop of flowers. The moss rose requires additional fertiliser only once per month.

Propagate via seeds.

> Aphids love to attack moss roses, so be sure to combat them as quickly as possible. Otherwise, they can damage the plants to such a degree that you will simply have to throw them away.

PRIMULA
Primrose

The name "Primula" means "first little one", since some species are among the earliest heralds of spring. The entire primrose family is named after this flower.

Of the more than 50 species of primrose, only a few are suitable as houseplants. However, an enormous assortment of cultivars exist among these few species. Primroses come from temperate zones, primarily Europe and China. They bloom abundantly, but most are short-lived. The leaves grow in a rosette formation close to the ground and are frequently hairy.

Place your primrose in a bright to semi-shady location; the flowers will last longer if it is cool. Keep the soil slightly moist at all times, but avoid standing water; fertilise very lightly. You can re-pot the longer-lasting German primrose after flowering and keep it cool over the winter at 10 to 12 °C (50–54 °F). Plant common primroses in the garden: they will bloom again the following year.

Species and Types

Primula malacoides, fairy primrose, baby primrose: in China, these grow along the edges of rice fields; a fragrant annual plant; flowers are single or compound, many colours. *P. obconica*, German or poison primrose: from central China. Its glandular hairs secrete a substance that contains primin; skin contact can cause allergic reactions. Primin-free varieties have been developed; many cultivated varieties with red, pink, white, blue or two-toned flowers. *P. vulgaris*, common or English primrose: many varieties, often with yellow centres; pillow-like leave cushions.

PTERIS
Brake fern, Cretan brake, Table fern

The entire brake family owes its name to this very interestingly shaped fern. The brake fern grows in the humid forests of the tropics and subtropics. Its subterraneous rhizomes give rise to decorative, feathery fronds. The undersides of its fertile fronds are lined with spore pods.

Green varieties of the brake fern prefer a cool, semi-shady location; winter temperatures should ideally be around 12 °C (54 °F). Coloured varieties like a location that is bright to semi-shady, at room temperature in summer and 16 to 18 °C (61–64 °F) in winter. All types require high humidity, soft, warm water and a lime-free substrate; they do not tolerate drafts well. Water moderately and evenly in summer, less in winter when temperatures are low. Fertilise lightly every two weeks from April to August, re-pot in spring.

Propagate by dividing carefully at the time of re-potting, or via spores.

Species and Types

Pteris cretica: the best-known species; robust, great variation; 'Wimsettii': light green, irregular, double feathers, curly leaf tips, hardy and easy to care for; 'Alblineata': wider feathers with a white central stripe; 'Roeweri': more thickly branching, bushy growth. *P. ensiformis:* a pretty little fern; 'Evergemiensis' has white-striped leaves; 'Victoriae'. *P. quadriaurita:* has double feathers; 'Argyraea' has greenish white stripes in the centre of the feathers. *P. tremula:* comes from New

Zealand and Australia; sturdy, grows up to 1 metre (3 ft) tall; has light green, triangular, feathered fronds.

RADERMACHERA SINICA
Radermachera, China doll

This decorative little indoor tree of the jacaranda family originates in China, where it grows to a tall tree with large sulphur-coloured, bell-shaped flowers. In our homes, the radermachera will grow to ca. 1.5 metres (5 ft) and does not produce flowers: it is a relatively new houseplant. Its evergreen, shiny, dark green leaves are doubly feathered, and their shape resembles those of an ash tree. The radermachera absolutely does not tolerate cigarette smoke.

Place this plant in a bright, airy spot away from direct sun. It prefers room temperature in summer and around 15 °C (59 °F) in winter. Keep the soil moist; water sparingly in winter. Fertilise every three weeks from March to August. Re-pot young plants every year, older ones every two to three; ensure the pot has good drainage. Propagate via seeds.

RANUNCULUS ASIATICUS
Ranunculus, Persian buttercup

The ranunculus is a winter-hardy plant, which makes it ideally suited for a balcony or patio. It can tolerate low temperatures—from 0 to 10 °C (32–50 °F)—very well. If the temperature drops below freezing it is best to move the plant into a corner that receives morning sun.

The ranunculus feels most comfortable in semi-shade, but will not complain even if it is placed in intense sunlight. On the other hand, it does not react favourably to wind at all. Ranunculus is a relatively undemanding plant: if you replace its substrate every year, you will only need to fertilise it sparingly. It is also quite forgiving when it comes to watering. You should allow the soil to become thoroughly dry between one watering and the next. Propagate via seeds or division in spring or autumn.

Species and Types
Ranunculus lanuginosus, R. ficaria, R. aconitifolius. 'Cardinal' has red flowers, 'Madonna' white, and 'Parisienne' has pink flowers.

REBUTIA
Rebutia

These delightful little cacti come from the area from northern Argentina to southern Bolivia, where they grow in the cracks of rocks and on dry steppes at altitudes up to 3,600 metres (11,800 ft). Rebutia grows to at most 8 cm (3 in); its ribs grow in a spiral form, ending in warts and sharp thorns. The cacti produce numerous sprouts from their bases and quickly form groups. The astonishingly big, brilliantly-coloured flowers arise not from the crown, but from the side of the plant, and often cover the entire cactus. Even the tiniest plants produce scarlet, yellow, orange or violet-pink flowers. Place your rebutia in a sunny, airy spot in front of a window, protected from direct midday sun. Keep it bright and cool in winter at around 5 °C (41 °F). Water normally in summer, little in spring and autumn, and not at all in winter. Supplement with cactus fertiliser ca. every three weeks in summer; mist on very hot days. Re-pot in loose, nutrient-rich soil only when needed. Propagate via seeds, which can even sow themselves, or division: rebutia is light-germinating.

Species and Types
Rebutia marsoneri: golden yellow flowers. *R. violaciflora*: violet. *R. senilis*: flattened ball shape, bright red flowers; white thorns, many varieties bloom in yellow, purple and orange. *R. miniscula*: 4 cm (1 ½ in) tall, scarlet flowers; 'Grandiflora' has very large blossoms. *R. pygmea*: a very tiny plant. *R. ritteri*: carmine red.

RECHSTEINERIA CARDINALIS
Cardinal flower

This pretty gesneriad, with its white-haired, light green leaves, is a native of Brazil. Its brilliant scarlet, tube-shaped flowers are arranged on flower axes. They usually bloom from June through August—sometimes as early as Mothers' Day.

As far as location and care are concerned, the cardinal flower's has the same needs as its close relative, the gloxinia. It requires semi-shade and a cool to room temperature location. It needs plenty of water during the growth period, as well as a dose of liquid fertiliser every two weeks. Gradually discontinue watering after the blooming period to allow the green parts of the plant to wither until autumn.

Keep the tubers in a cool, dry place (12–15 °C/54–59 °F) over the winter; re-pot them in fresh soil in spring and allow to sprout at 18 to 25 °C (64–77 °F); increase watering and fertilising.

Propagate by dividing the tubers in spring or via cuttings.

As is true of other plants whose leaves are covered with fine hairs, you will not help your cardinal flower by misting it to add humidity to the air. In fact, the attractive fuzz will suffer from too much moisture and, in the worst case, the leaves will develop unsightly blemishes.

RHAPIS
Lady palm

The attractive lady palm, which is native to China and Japan, was already popular in Europe around the turn of the 20th century. Its slender, bamboo-like stalks are covered with brown filaments; the leaves are 15 to 30 cm (6–12 in) wide and feathered in a fan formation. You can cultivate the lady palm as a single palm or as a bonsai.

Find the lady palm a bright to semi-shady—but not sunny—location. In summer it also enjoys a draft-free spot outdoors. Keep it warm in summer, cool (5–10 °C/41–50 °F) in winter. Water generously in spring and summer, more sparingly in the winter. Mist the plant often with soft water. Fertilise lightly once a week in summer. Re-pot as needed. Propagate via seeds or offshoots.

Species

Rhapis humilis: grows up to a metre (3 ft) tall; its feathered leaves are narrower and more delicate and numerous. *R. excelsa*: grows up to 2 metres (7 ft) tall; leaves are divided into five to seven feathers.

RHIPSALIDOPSIS
Easter cactus

The Easter cactus, which is similar to the orchid cactus and the Christmas cactus, originates in the tropical forests of southern Brazil, where it lives on trees as an epiphyte. It is a jointed cactus—that is,

> Understandably, flower lovers would like to increase the number of radiant, scarlet blossoms on their Easter cacti even more. However, turning the plant toward the light as often as possible is the wrong approach, since it may cause the joints to drop off. Too much water is also disadvantageous: it can result in root rot.

it has evenly jointed, flat shoots which, in spring, bear the brilliantly coloured flowers at their tips. The Easter cactus has thickly branching, overhanging stems and weak roots. It requires a warm, bright to semi-shady location with high humidity and does not like to be rotated. Water generously with soft water during the growing period; supplement with cactus fertiliser two to three times. Water very sparingly during the rest period. Keep the plant cool in winter to encourage blooming the following year. Re-pot as needed in low-lime, humus-ruch soil. May is best time to

propagate (after blooming), using single joints.

Species

Rhipsalidopsis gaertneri: has many branches; scarlet flowers with long, pointed petals that curl back somewhat. *R. rosea:* fragrant pink flowers. *R. x graeseri:* a cross between the two previously mentioned species; flowers are pink to violet. This species should be kept in a bright and relatively warm location, even in the winter. However, if the substrate is less moist, they will tolerate temperatures as low as 8 °C (46 °F).

RHODODENDRON
Indian Azalea, Rhododendron

Rhododendron simsii, a member of the heather family originating in East Asia, is a

small shrub with luxurious blossoms. Its botanical name means "rose tree". Its small, evergreen leaves are leathery and have coarse hair on the undersides. Depending on the variety, azaleas bloom from winter until spring; they often arrive in our homes as potted plants at Christmastime. The attractive flowers are not fragrant, but come in many colours and shapes—single and compound, white to dark red. The azalea feels at home in locations similar to its native habitat in the brisk, cool and humid mountain forests. It will not flourish long in warm dry air. Place the plant in a shady location outdoors from May through September. Water generously in summer, less at other times; use softened water or water that has been allowed to stand. Never let the root ball dry out, but avoid standing water. Fertilise every two weeks with azalea fertiliser, from the end of the blooming period until late July. Remove wilted blossoms, prune some and re-pot every two years in a special lime-free azalea substrate.

Other Species

Rhododendron obtusum, the Japanese azalea, is more robust, has small flowers, and is well suited to bonsai cultivation.

RHOEO SPATHACEA
Moses-in-the-cradle, Oyster plant, Boat lily

This imposing member of the spiderwort family comes from the tropics of Central America. The plant's sword-shaped leaves, which can grow up to 30 cm (12 in) long, grow diagonally upwards. They are olive green on the surface and dark red to violet on the undersides, and stand side by side in a rosette-like formation. A short trunk develops in older plants.

The plant's descriptive names refer to its boat or pocket-shaped spathes, which rest at the base of its lower leaves, with the tiny white flowers peeking up in between them.

Place your Moses-in-the-cradle in a semi-shady location at room temperature all year round. The plant requires high humidity, particularly in summer.

Keep the soil slightly moist with soft, room temperature water in the summer; water less in the winter. Fertilise every week from March through August; mist frequently. Re-pot in spring if necessary.

Propagate via side or top runners, or via seeds.

Type

'Vittata': leaves have yellowish-white, vertical stripes.

ROSA CHINENSIS
Chinese rose, Bengal rose, Miniature rose

Roses are atypical houseplants, since we are otherwise accustomed to seeing them in gardens.

The only roses that are truly appropriate for indoor cultivation are the descendants of the Chinese rose *Rosa chinensis* 'Minima' (*Rosa rouletii*), of which there are many cultivars. They may be single or compound, grow between 25 cm and 40 cm (10–15 in) tall, and bloom in many different colours.

Potted roses like the same treatment as garden roses. Your Chinese rose will thrive in an airy, bright to sunny location—outdoors in summer, if possible. Always cut off wilted leaves or flowers. Keep it frost-free over the winter, at ca. 5 °C (41 °F).

Keep the soil moist from spring until autumn; in winter, water just enough that the root ball does not dry out. Fertilise every two weeks from March to mid-August.

Prune the plant back and re-pot in spring. Propagate via cuttings or seeds.

Types

'Zwergkönig' (red) and 'Zwergkönigin' (pink), 'Baby Maskerade' (orange-yellow), 'Colibri' (red), 'Rosina' (yellow), 'Pour Toi' (white), 'Muttertag' (deep red).

SAINTPAULIA IONANTHA
African violet

The African violet was first discovered by Walter von Saint Paul-Illaire near the end of the nineteenth century, in the tropical forests of East Africa's Usambara Mountains. In a short time it became one of our most popular houseplants. It is no relation to the European violet, but is rather a member of the gesneriad family. The flowers—originally violet-blue—grow on thin stems and look very pretty against the background of the plant's fuzzy, dark green leaves. African violets fit in almost anywhere: on windows as well as in the centre of a room; they look very attractive when placed together in a large group. When well cared-for, African violets will bloom tirelessly throughout the year, but they are well served by a month's rest period in winter.

African violets like to be comfortably warm all year round; the location should be bright to semi-shady, but not sunny, with sufficient humidity. Keep the soil uniformly moist with soft, pleasantly warm water. Water the plant below its rosette of leaves, or better still, in its saucer. Remove any excess water after 30 minutes, since they do not tolerate wet feet. Do not mist; pluck out any wilted blossoms. Fertilise lightly once a week in spring and summer; re-pot every spring. Propagation is usually carried out via leaf cuttings; larger plants may also be divided.

Types

A vast assortment is available in every shade from white to red to blue. Multi-coloured, single, compound, curly and small-blossom varieties have all been cultivated.

SALVIA SPLENDENS
Salvia, Scarlet sage

Chefs love to keep aromatic sage in their herb gardens; lovers of bright colours are thrilled by the intense red of *Salvia splendens* in a pot or flower box. In European latitudes the salvia—which is actually a perennial—should be treated as an annual. The first frost brings an end to the spectacular beauty of its upright inflorescences, which consist of both flowers and bracts. Also be absolutely certain there is no danger of frost before planting the salvia in spring. In general, you can reckon on blooming that lasts from June through September. The salvia is happiest with a location in full sunlight; it will grudgingly accept very bright shade.

Water generously, especially when several salvia plants are placed together in a single container. Fertilise every ten days. If you remove the wilted flower axes immediately, the salvia will bloom several times.

Propagate in spring via seeds or division.

Types

'Weissfeuer', 'Johannisfeuer', 'Feuerzauber'.

Aphids feel very much at home in the juicy tips of the salvia's branches. Shield bugs, on the other hand, make small, zigzag-shaped holes in the leaves. Once you have successfully combatted any pests, cut off the dead sections of the plant.

SANSEVIERIA TRIFASCIATA

Snake plant, Sansevieria, Mother-in-law's tongue, Good luck plant

This member of the agave family from the African deserts is one of our most tenacious houseplants. In its native countries, it was cultivated for its hemp-like fibres (it is also called viper's bowstring hemp). Its stiff, stemless leaves are elegantly patterned and end in sharp points. They can store water in their interiors, allowing this desert plant to survive long dry seasons. The snake plant is undemanding, vigorous and grows tirelessly. Its root stalk will handily crack apart a container that becomes too small for it. The plant occasionally produces delicate, fragrant, greenish-white flowers. The snake plant can tolerate dry or polluted air, making it a good plant for businesses, restaurants or offices, but it should be placed in a sunny location. The decorative leaf patterns fade if the location is too dark. Water sparingly; supplement with low-nitrogen fertiliser every two to four weeks. Re-pot once a year; larger plants every two years. These plants are more comfortable in shallow containers. Propagation is usually carried out via division. Leaf cuttings always produce green offspring.

Types

'Laurentii': the best-known variety; tall-growing with yellow-edged leaves; also known as mother-in-law's tongue. 'Hahnii': low-growing leaf rosettes. 'Golden Hahnii': like the previous type, but with yellow vertical stripes.

SAXIFRAGA STOLONIFERA

Creeping saxifrage, Strawberry begonia, Roving sailor

This member of the saxifrage family, which grows in a rosette-like formation, is native to China and Japan. Countless plantlets develop on its long, thread-like runners or stolons, (hence its Latin name). The leaves—which, like the runners, have red stems—are round to kidney-shaped with slightly wavy lobes, dark green with white veins on the surface and dotted with red on the underside. There are also coloured-leaf varieties. White, star-shaped flowers may appear in panicles in summer. Creeping saxifrage requires a bright to semi-shady, airy location. In summer it may be outdoors. The plant also tolerates cooler temperatures, particularly in winter; however, coloured-leaf varieties require temperatures of at least 15 °C (59 °F). Keep the soil moderately moist; water less if the plant is kept cool for the winter. Fertilise every week or two in summer; re-pot in spring.

Propagate using the runner plantlets, which have often already formed roots: you need only set them in the soil.

Types

'Tricolor': green leaves with edges that are initially rose-coloured, later white.

SCAEVOLA
Scaevola, Fanflower

Are you looking for another intense blue or purple shade for your flower arrangements? The native Australian scaevola, an annual plant with cascading blossoms, will leave the competition in the dust. Its modest leaves are completely obscured behind its brilliant, luxuriant flowers. The scaevola's overhanging branches, which can grow up to a metre (3 ft) long, look just as beautiful in a hanging basket as they do in a window box or a pot placed on a high shelf. The scaevola produces particularly abundant blossoms when placed in direct sunlight, but it will tolerate a semi-shady location without any complaints. Water moderately: it is enough to simply keep the plant moist. Avoid standing water. From late spring until into the autumn, the scaevola requires a light dose of fertiliser every week.

Propagation via cuttings is difficult.

SCHEFFLERA
Umbrella tree

These tropical members of the aralia family are named after eighteenth-century botanist Jakob Christian Scheffler. They have large, hand-shaped leaves: the number of "spokes" in the umbrellas increases as they mature. These fast-growing plants are trees in their natural habitat. In the home, their effect is most attractive if they stand alone in a large room. They are also excellent plants for hydroponic cultivation.

Umbrella trees require a bright to semi-shady location that receives fresh air, but no drafts. Keep the plant at room temperature or cooler; in the summer, it may go outdoors. The location may be cooler in winter, but plants with variegated leaves require temperatures of at least 12 to 16 °C (54–61 °F). Water moderately in summer and fertilise every two weeks; water sparingly in winter. Repot in spring.

Propagation via seeds is the most successful method.

Species

Schefflera actinophylla: the best-known species, it is being re-named as *Brassaia actinophylla*; originates in Australia; its long-stemmed, shiny, leathery leaves grow up to 30 cm (12 in) wide. *S. arboricola*, more delicate, smaller leaves; variegated types are newer.

SCHLUMBERGERA
Christmas cactus

The winter-blooming Christmas cactus originally comes from the tropical rainforests of Brazil, where it grows epiphytically on trees. It is densely branched and has overhanging stems. Its flowers, which are symmetrical on two sides, radiate in many enchanting colours.

The Christmas cactus requires a semi-shady location; you may place it outdoors in summer, but move it to a warm place at the end of September. Mist frequently; do not rotate. The plant requires a rest period after the blooming phase. Keep the soil moderately moist with soft, plea-

santly warm water during the growth period; supplement with cactus fertiliser every two weeks. Water sparingly in autumn and winter. Re-pot in spring, after the rest period. Propagate via cuttings (with mature joints).

Types

Countless hybrids in every colour from white to purplish-red; 'Gold Charm' is yellow.

> Like the Easter cactus, the Christmas cactus does not like to be rotated often and will not tolerate frequent changes of location: it reacts by losing its flowers and buds.

SCINDAPSUS PICTUS
Satin pothos, Pothos vine, Silver vine

The satin pothos, a climbing plant of the arum lily family, is a native of Southeast Asia. Its heart-shaped, somewhat asymmetrical leaves are dark green with light speckles. Its hanging and climbing growth pattern makes it an attractive hanging plant; it is perfect for an enclosed plant window. The pothos is also easy to maintain hydroponically.

The satin pothos requires a very warm, bright to semi-shady location with warm soil and high humidity throughout the year.

Keep the soil moderately moist with soft, pleasantly warm water in summer; water somewhat less in winter; mist often! The pothos needs to be fertilised every week from March through September; re-pot as necessary, every two to three years.

Propagate via cuttings.

Types

'Argyraeus': its green leaves are speckled and edged in silver.

143

SCIRPUS CERNUUS
Fibre optic grass, Fibre optic rush

This pretty sedge, with its fresh green tufts, 20 to 25 cm (8–10 in) tall, originates in the Mediterranean region. Tiny white flower heads, the size pinheads, form at the tips of its delicate reeds. In its natural habitat, the bulrush stands upright; in our homes, it bends over slightly, making it a beautiful plant for a hanging basket. It is also excellently suited to hydroponics. Unfortunately, in recent years, it has frequently been marketed as a "grass tree", unnaturally forced to grow inside narrow tubes.

The fibre optic rush prefers a bright to semi-shady—but not sunny—location with high humidity; it requires room temperature conditions throughout the year.

Unlike most other plants, the fibre optic rush—originally a marsh plant—loves having "wet feet". Therefore, water it generously: it is good to leave a little water in the saucer; however, the entire root ball should not stand under water. Fertilise lightly in summer; re-pot in spring.

Propagate via seeds in spring or via division when re-potting, separating the outermost sections of the plant.

SEDUM
Sedum, stonecrop

The botanical name of this delightful plant comes from the Latin *sedare* (to keep off). The ancient Romans placed these plants on the roofs of their houses to ward off lightening. Sedums store moisture in their thick leaves and are well known as rock garden plants. The species that we cultivate as houseplants originated in Mexico. They have their growth period in the summer and make very attractive plants for pots or hanging baskets.

The sedum's location should be bright and sunny, warm to moderately warm in summer: you can even place it in a sheltered location outdoors. In the winter, keep the plant cool, if possible.

Water very moderately in summer, using lukewarm water; even less in winter. Re-pot as necessary, preferably in cactus substrate.

Propagate via division or cuttings. Allow the cut-off edges to dry for several days before setting them in the soil.

Species and Types

Sedum morganianum, donkey's tail: a striking hanging plant with shoots that hang down over the edges of the pot and can be several metres long; mottled grey-green, fleshy leaves; very fragile to the touch. With luck, it will produce rose-coloured flowers. *S. pachyphyllum*, jellybean plant: thick, fleshy leaves turn upwards; blue-green with red tips. *S. rubro-tinctum*: thick, fleshy leaves, green to red-brown; yellow flowers. *S. sieboldii*, 'Okto-berle': flowers pink in autumn; leaves less thick; cultivate in a cool place; 'Medio-variegatum': leaves have red edges and yellow spots.

SENECIO CRUENTUS
Cineraria

The prototype for this delightful composite-flower plant makes its home in the mountains of the Canary Islands. They come in many colours, large and small, one and two-toned flowers, with and without "eyes".

The name cineraria comes from Latin *cinerarius* ("ashen"), reference to the bluish-grey down on the undersides of the leaves. It has also been called "aphid plant", since they are highly attracted to it. The cineraria's main flowering period is in early spring; it begins in the late winter.

Cineraria needs a cool, bright and airy location, but not full sunlight. Water generously, fertilise weekly and provide indirect humidity when possible. Do not mist the leaves directly, since it is vulnerable to mildew and botrytis blight. Unfortunately, the cineraria is an annual and will wither after the blooming period. Propagation via seeds is difficult.

Types

Cinerarias are available in many beautiful colours.

> The nickname "aphid plant" is well justified: overly high temperatures provide ideal conditions for these pests. Excessive humidity can also lead to mildew attacks.

SETCREASEA PURPUREA
Wandering Jew, Purple heart

The wandering Jew, a member of the spiderwort family, originates in the highlands of Mexico. It is a close relative of tradescantia, or spiderwort, with which it is often confused.

The entire plant is violet-purple and the leaves have bluish mottling on their surface. The flowers are pale purple and inconspicuous. Its hanging growth pattern makes the wandering Jew an ideal candidate for hanging pots.

Place the plant in a very bright spot if you wish to preserve the interesting leaf colouring. It does not require a lot of warmth. Keep the soil moist; do not water the leaves. Fertilise lightly once per week from March through August. Re-pot in spring, or better yet, regenerate the plant with cuttings. These are easy to root at any time of year.

Types

'Purple heart': this pretty plant is the only variety.

SINNINGIA
Gloxinia, Sinningia

The tropic gesneriad *Sinningia speciosa* is native to the Brazilian rainforests.

Both its sumptuous, bell-shaped flowers and its large leaves feel velvety to the touch. They bloom from March through August. The colourful, newly cultivated varieties are enjoying ever-increasing popularity.

Gloxinias require bright, consistently warm conditions with high humidity. They grow particularly well in hothouses. Protect your plant from drafts and direct sunlight.

Water gloxinias regularly below the leaves, with soft, pleasantly warm water; do not mist. Fertilise lightly once a week or even more often. Water less at the end of the summer.

Allow the tubers to dry out in the autumn and store them over winter in their old soil at about 15 °C (59 °F); re-pot in the spring.

Types

Countless hybrids exist, in numerous colours ranging from white to red to blue, as well as multi-coloured, single and compound flowers. The plant's original colour was violet-purple; 'Sonnenuntergang' has dark red flowers.

SOLANUM PSEUDOCAPSICUM
Jerusalem cherry

This charming, South American member of the nightshade family is a poisonous, evergreen semi-shrub whose flowers resemble those of the potato plant. In autumn the blossoms develop into shiny, bright orange to scarlet, spherical fruits, which will last until February if the plant is kept in a cool location.

Place Jerusalem cherry in a bright, sunny, airy and moderately warm spot: sunshine is essential for proper development of the flowers and fruit. Keep the plant outdoors in summer, if possible, to allow for pollination. In winter, keep it at 7 to 10 °C (44–50 °F).

Water generously during the growth period, only a little during the rest phase; fertilise every two weeks in summer. Prune the plant back and re-pot before it begins producing new growth in spring.

Propagate via seeds: remove the fleshy part of the fruit, allow the seeds to dry out and sow them in spring.

Other Species and Types

Solanum capsicastrum: bears smaller, red fruits; 'Variegatum' has white and multi-coloured leaves. *S. melongena*, eggplant tree: a white variation of the aubergine; an annual. *S. aviculare*, kangaroo apple: has pale violet flowers; comes from New Zealand and Australia. *S. jasminoides*, potato vine: may also be cultivated as a climbing plant. *S. laciniatum*, cut-leaved nightshade: grows up to 3 metres (10 ft) tall with violet flowers.

SOLEIROLIA SOLEIROLII
Mind-your-own-business, Dandy, Baby's tears

This pretty member of the nettle family, native to Corsica, was previously known by the botanical name *Helxine*. Its new name honours a captain named Soleirol. Because of its delicate, shiny little leaves, it is often called baby's tears.

This low, pale green plant grows in a ball shape and works well in both pots and hanging baskets in the home. In its homeland in sunny southern Europe, mind-your-own-business grows out of cracks in walls or rocks and energetically produces new growth after a mild winter. It flourishes in partial shade, protected from the blazing sun. It likes to be cool but will tolerate room temperature. Since it requires high humidity, mist the plant often. Water moderately but regularly; never allow the soil to dry out. Fertilise occasionally in the summer if the plant is not growing well. It is possible to keep mind-your-own-business over the winter; however, you will obtain stronger plants by propagating them via division.

Propagation with cuttings is also possible: even the tiniest segments of this plant will form roots and continue to grow.

Types

'Argentea' silver, 'Aurea' has golden-green leaves.

SPARMANNIS AFRICANA
African hemp, African linden

This abundantly branching South African shrub is a member of the linden family, just like our common linden tree. With its large, fluffy-haired, linden-green leaves, the African hemp is a houseplant with a long tradition in Europe. It grows quite quickly and requires a great deal of space as it gets older. In the spring it will sometimes produce pretty white flowers with yellow and red filaments.

The African hemp prefers a bright, airy and moderately warm location, well protected from drafts. It can be placed outdoors in summer; it needs a cool rest period from October through December.

Water generously during the growth period and fertilise weekly; water sparingly in the rest phase. Re-pot young plants at least once a year; older plants only when necessary.

Propagate by means of flower-bearing cuttings, if possible; cultivate them in a heated propagating case.

> The African hemp is highly decorative but far from simple to care for: it is sensitive to gases, smoke and coal dust. If it lacks light, water or nutrients, it will react by losing its leaves. In addition, it is susceptible to pests such as spider mites, thrips, white flies and aphids.

SPATHIPHYLLUM
Peace lily

This elegant member of the arum lily family is native to tropical America and the Indian archipelago. Its white to greenish-white, leaf-like spathe surrounding a cream-coloured spadix is distinctive; the inflorescence is very long-lasting. The peace lily's leaves are long, lancet-shaped, non-segmented, evergreen and glossy. This plant is particularly suited to hydroponics.

The peace lily prefers semi-shade to shade at room temperature throughout the year. It requires high humidity in summer; in winter, it should not be kept cooler than 16 °C (61 °F).

Keep soil moist with softened, room temperature water; somewhat less in winter; mist on warm days. Fertilise lightly every two weeks from March to August; re-pot in spring. Propagate via division at the time of re-potting.

Species and Types
Spathiphyllum floribundum: best-known species; 30 to 40 cm (12–15 in) tall; flowers are long-lasting and may be used as cut flowers. *S. wallisii:* spathe turns green quickly; 'Mauna Loa' is a fragrant variety. *S. patinii:* 'Marion Wagner', 'Clevelandii' and 'McCoy' varieties are 60 to 80 cm (24–30 in) tall.

STAPELIA GRANDIFLORA
Stapelia, Carrion plant, Starfish flower

The stapelia, a member of the milkweed family, originates in the dry regions of South, Southwest and East Africa. Its short, fat, four-sided stems are grey-green and fleshy. Its magnificent, unique, 10 to 15 cm (4–6 in) wide star-shaped flowers emit an obnoxious, carrion-like odour. The smell attracts carrion flies, which pollinate the plant. Not all species have an equally intense smell. The stapelia also makes a very interesting hanging plant. It is an undemanding plant: in summer, it is happy outdoors, on a sunny windowsill or in a greenhouse. Its location should be warm, airy and very bright, but protected from direct sun.

In winter, the stapelia likes very bright and cool conditions, at temperatures of 5 to 10 °C (41–50 °F). It is not harmed by dry air.

Water the plant with water that has been allowed to stand: sparingly in the summer and even less in winter (once per month). Fertilise lightly every three weeks in summer; if you re-pot the plant every year, you will not need to fertilise at all. Propagate via seeds or cuttings, allowing the cut-off edges to dry out before planting.

Species
Stapelia gigantea: flowers are 25 to 35 cm (10–14 in) wide. *S. variegata:* brown-spotted flowers, 5 to 8 cm (2–3 in) wide.

STEPHANOTIS FLORIBUNDA
Madagascar jasmine, Bridal wreath, Stephanotis

This evergreen climbing shrub from the mountains of Madagascar is a member of the milkweed family. Its white, wonderfully aromatic, star-shaped flowers with their trumpet-shaped coronas bloom from April to August and are arranged together on umbels. Its dark green leaves are shiny and leathery. Its tough, metres-long branches are flexible and strong: they require an arch, trellis or wall on which they can climb.

Place your Madagascar jasmine in an airy, bright, but not sunny location that is warm in summer and cool (12–14 °C/ 54–57 °F) in the winter. Do not rotate the plant or change its location! Water it generously with soft, room temperature water from March through August, less later in the year; keep the soil only slightly moist in winter. Fertilise every one or two weeks from March through August; mist the leaves occasionally. Re-pot in spring if necessary. Propagate from spring right through the fall using cuttings placed in a heated propagating case.

The Madagascar jasmine is every bit as sensitive as its name suggests. If kept too warm in winter it is at greater risk for spider mites, mealybugs and scale insects. It reacts to a change in location by losing its buds and flowers. This beautiful specimen will develop yellow leaves if given over-hard water or deprived of light.

STRELITZIA REGINAE
Bird of paradise, Crane flower

A species of bird of paradise, a plant native to South Africa, has recently become available as a house or container plant. With its spectacular, exotic flowers, this plant has played a more important role up to now as a cut flower. Its name can be traced back to Charlotte Sophia von Mecklenburg Strelitz. The plant can grow up to 1.5 metres (5 ft) high. Its bluish-green, leathery, long-stemmed leaves resemble those of the banana tree—a clue that the bird of paradise is a member of the banana family. Its symmetrical flowers, which are supported by reddish-green, boat-shaped spathes, emerge from diagonally-growing sheathes; they appear in the winter and spring. The individual flowers can grow up to 15 cm (6 in) long and are made up of three outer, narrow, lancet-shaped orange petals; the sky blue inner petals protrude out of the flower like arrows.

The bird of paradise should be placed in a bright and sunny location; in the summer, it is best to place it outdoors. In the house, the plant prefers moderate temperatures and plenty of fresh air. Water it moderately and fertilise every two weeks during the vegetation period. In winter, the bird of paradise needs to be kept cool, at 8 to 15 °C (46–59 °F); keep the root ball moist with pleasantly warm water.

Propagate via seeds or by dividing older plants in spring. Seed-grown plants will require up to four years before they produce their first flowers.

STREPTOCARPUS
Cape primrose, Streptocarpus

This attractive gesneriad is native to parts of Africa, Madagascar, Thailand and Burma, where it grows on the floors of mountain forests. The Greek name *streptocarpus* means "twisted fruit", a reference to the plant's fruit capsules, which are twisted into a spiral. Its elongated, funnel-shaped flowers are asymmetrical, and come in every shade of white, red and blue. There are two-toned varieties, as well as types with patterned throats or curly edges. The tongue-shaped, wrinkly leaves grow in a rosette and are remarkably big. The Cape primrose requires room temper-ature year round and partial shade out of direct sun. Keep the soil evenly moist with

soft, room temperature water; don't water the leaves. Provide indirect humidity in summer and fertilise every week or two. Re-pot in spring. This plant is sensitive to smoke, drafts, and changes in location. The best method of propagation is via leaf cuttings in spring. It can also be divided at the time of re-potting or propagated with seeds.

Species and Types

Streptocarpus wendlandii: a bizarre plant with one giant leaf up to 90 cm (3 ft) long; dark olive green on the surface, purple-red underneath; bears ca. 30 violet blossoms. *S. saxorum*: a hanging plant with small flowers. *Streptocarpus* hybrids, e.g. the purple 'Constant-Nymph'.

STROMANTHE AMABILIS
Stromanthe

This striking member of the prayer plant family comes from the tropics of South America. It is often confused with the closely related genera *Ctenanthe* and *Calathea*. Its beautiful oval leaves are green on the surface, decorated with greyish-white diagonal stripes. The stromanthe flourishes in a location that is semi-shady and warm all year round, with high humidity—an enclosed plant window is ideal. Water generously with soft water; don't let the root ball dry out, but avoid wet feet as well; mist daily. Fertilise every one or two weeks in summer, once per month in the winter; re-pot in spring. Propagate via division at the time of re-potting.

Other Species

Stromanthe sanguinea: elongated leaves with dark green and white patterns on the surface, undersides purplish-red. *S. porteana*: whitish-green leaves with silver veins.

> The stromanthe's leaves can be damaged by mistakes made in its care, such as over-hard water or dry air. You can successfully propagate it via top cuttings as well as by division.

SYNGONIUM
Arrowhead vine, African evergreen, Nephthytis

The arrowhead vine, which comes from the tropical rain forests of South and Central America, is frequently confused with the philodendron.

But unlike other members of the arum lily family, the arrowhead vine contains milky sap. Older plants produce greenish arum lily flowers, whose flower sheath glows purplish-red on the inside. Its shiny green or mottled leaves change in time: in their young stage they are arrow-shaped; later they become increasingly lobed and segmented. Aerial roots form on the leaf nodes, which may be guided into the earth. The arrowhead vine can climb, hang or creep: it is ideal for a hanging basket or a trellis. It also does well in hydroponic culture.

The arrowhead vine's location needs to be warm (above 18 °C/64 °F) with warm soil; high humidity is essential to its survival. Place coloured-leaf varieties in a bright, but not sunny, location; green varieties like a bright to semi-shady spot.

Keep the soil slightly but consistently moist with soft, room temperature water. Mist the plant often and wipe the leaves with a damp cloth. As soon as new shoots appear, fertilise each week or two. Re-pot every one to two years.

Propagate via cuttings planted in a heated propagating case.

Species

Syngonium podophyllum: the most common species; green and attractively patterned coloured-leaf varieties. *S. vellozianum:* closely resembles the philodendron; green.

TAGETES ERECTA
Marigold

It is hard to find a patio or garden that does not include the annual marigold, with its cheerful yellow and orange flowers that bloom abundantly until the first frost. Along with the pelargonium, it is simply part of the standard repertoire—not only because of its appearance, but probably because you don't need a particularly green thumb to achieve beautiful results with this flower.

When purchasing seeds, you should keep the future height of the plants in mind: marigolds can be found in heights

ranging from 30 to 80 cm (12–30 in). This robust plant makes no special demands as far as light conditions are concerned: it blossoms as prettily and luxuriantly in the shade as it does in the sun. Nor does wind pose a danger to marigolds.

The marigold responds well to generous watering—even twice a day in very hot weather. You can fertilise the plants once per week.

Propagate via seeds.

Types

'Vanilla', 'Crackerjack', 'Discovery'.

THUNBERGIA ALATA
Black-eyed Susan vine, Clock vine

Black-eyed Susan, one of our most popular climbing plants, can flourish both inside the house or on a patio, where it will bloom from the early summer until well into the autumn. Its petals, which lie flat around the black central eye, can be found in every shade of white, yellow or orange.

Black-eyed Susan definitely requires a climbing support, be it posts, wires or a trellis. With this kind of help, it can reach a maximum height of 2 metres (7 ft). Both annual varieties as well as perennial and winter-hardy types are available.

Black-eyed Susan thrives best in a warm location in full sunlight.

Water the plant frequently during the blooming period; hard water will not harm it. Fertilise every two weeks. If you prune your black-eyed Susan strategically, you can create a compact, bushy shape.

Propagate via seeds.

TILLANDSIA
Tillandsia, Spanish moss, Ball moss

This most extensive genus of the bromeliad family is native to South America and southern North America, where the plants can be found in a variety of habitats. There are two groups: green tillandsias live epiphytically and develop true roots; the grey varieties have narrow, grass-like leaves densely covered with silver-grey absorbent scales through which the plant absorbs moisture and nutrients. These plants have no true roots; rather, they attach themselves to trees or rocks with clinging roots. They can even survive dry spells, taking in their fill of moisture again afterwards. Green tillandsias need a warm, bright to semi-shady location, protected from direct sunlight. They need high humidity and a mix of pine needles, crushed dried leaves, sand and swamp moss as a substrate. These varieties grow best in a warm, humid plant window.

Grey tillandsias like warm, airy, bright or even sunny conditions. They can be outdoors in a sheltered place; in winter, they should be kept between 10 and 15 °C (50–59 °F). Set your plant in some sphagnum on an epiphyte stalk and secure well.

All tillandsias prefer soft water, which you should pour directly into the leaf funnels or mist onto the plant's leaves. Add a weak dose of fertiliser to the water every two weeks.

Propagate via offshoots.

Species
Tillandsia cyanea: blue-green leaf rosettes; the inflorescence is made up of double rows of rose-coloured spathes from which single blue-violet flowers emerge. *T. lindenii* is similar in appearance to the previous species. *T. usneoides*, Louisiana moss, is grey with absorbent scales and resembles a beard lichen; in its native home, it drapes over trees or poles where it absorbs rainwater and becomes very heavy.

TOLMIEA MENZIESII
Piggyback plant, Youth-on-age, Mother of thousands

This charming member of the stonecrop family from the western part of North America has an interesting characteristic: tiny young plants continuously spring up on the surface of its heart-shaped leaves, which bear glandular hairs. The plantlets form roots as soon as the parent leaf leans down towards the soil. The piggyback plant is very easy to care for. It makes an excellent hanging plant, but it also works well as a pot plant or a groundcover for a winter garden.

Place your piggyback plant in partial shade, but not sun. It likes cool and airy conditions but will tolerate room temperature. In summer it will thrive on a patio or outdoors.

Water moderately to generously depending on the temperature. If you keep the plant at room temperature, mist it frequently. Fertilise once a week in spring and summer.

Propagate via plantlets: simply set them on the ground, with or without the parent leaf. Robust plants may also be divided.

TRACHYCARPUS FORTUNEI
Windmill palm, Chusan palm, Chinese fan palm

The Chinese windmill palm, which is frequently confused with the Mediterranean fan palm, is a native of Southeast Asia. However, the windmill palm differs in that its long leaf stems are flat and non-serrated. Its trunk is covered with sturdy fibres that form at the base of the fronds; these fall off gradually over the course of time. The windmill palm can grow up to 15 metres (50 ft) tall in its natural habitat; as a houseplant, it remains much smaller. The palm produces six to eight new leaves per year. Their deeply notched fronds remain fresh for several years.

The windmill palm loves a bright, airy location: in summer, it can be placed in a sunny spot outdoors. It is cold-resistant and will even tolerate light frost.

Keep the soil consistently moist; do not water into the "heart" of the tree.

Propagate via seeds.

> In the same way that the windmill palm can adapt to life in frosty mountain regions as well as to milder vineyards, it also takes re-potting very much in stride. You will only need to do this every three to five years. Do not expect the plant to produce flowers until it is quite a few years old.

TRADESCANTIA
Spiderwort, Bluejacket, Purple heart, Purple queen

Members of the spiderwort family are known for rapid growth. Some varieties have attractive flowers; others are inconspicuous. This very popular American foliage plant family includes many species and is known for beautifully coloured and patterned leaves. The plants are easy to care for, with no special demands. With branches that hang over or lie on the ground, spiderwort is ideal as a hanging plant or as a groundcover.

Green-leaved plants like a bright location; coloured-leaf varieties like it very bright but not sunny. Keep all spiderworts at room temperature, somewhat cooler in winter.

Water moderately but regularly with warm water; keep your plant drier in winter. Fertilise weekly in summer. Cultivating new cuttings is more successful than re-potting, and is very easy: the cuttings form roots readily. Drafts can cause the plant to lose its leaves.

Species and Types

Tradescantia albiflora: vertically striped leaves; 'Rochford's Silver' and 'Albovittata': white flowers with silver stripes; 'Tricolor' has three-coloured leaves; 'Aureo vittata' has yellowish leaves. *T. blossfeldiana*: hairy; undersides of the leaves are red; 'Variegata': leaves are green tinged with creamy white and pink. *T. fluminensis*: 'Quicksilver' and 'Variegata': white and green stripes. *T. pallida*: 'Purple Heart' has dark violet branches.

The spiderwort blooms from April through September, is extremely easy to care for and simple to propagate.

TROPAEOLUM MAJUS CULTIVAR
Nasturtium, Indian cress

The nasturtium, a native of South America, can grow unusually large within just a few weeks. It's idea for filling in balcony boxes or containers that may initially look a little bare. Nasturtiums can hang down decoratively or—with a little help—grow upright.

In the same way, nasturtiums are a perfect choice for planting in newly dug flowerbeds or borders which may still contain some bare spots in the first year.

The nasturtium's large flowers gleam in every shade of yellow and red. Pay attention when purchasing seeds: there are small species that just clear the ground as well as climbing varieties which can easily become several metres high.

A location in direct sunlight will best stimulate optimum growth. Water generously. Fertiliser, applied in two-week cycles, is not necessary until the late summer.

Nasturtiums also have one very special characteristic: the flowers are edible and may be used as a colourful garnish for your meals.

Propagate via seeds.

VANDA COERULEA
Vanda, Blue orchid

The epiphytical vanda, a genus found in the monsoon regions of the Near East and New Guinea, is a very unusual colour for an orchid. Its fragrant flowers are light blue to pale violet, up to 13 cm (5 in) tall, and grow in loosely arranged groups of up to 20 blossoms. Its leathery, slightly fleshy leaves are evergreen. The vanda can grow over a metre (3 ft) tall, and its aerial roots are especially long.

The vanda is best suited to a hothouse: it requires a bright location (away from the blazing midday sun in summer) with high humidity and plenty of fresh air; it should be kept somewhat cooler at night and in winter.

Water generously with warm, soft water during the growing period, supplementing with diluted orchid fertiliser at every third watering; water less in winter. Re-pot as necessary, approximately every three years, ideally in an orchid basket.

Propagate using runners that have formed roots.

Species and Type

'Rothschildiana': 10-cm (4-in) flowers, violet-blue with very dark veins. *Vanda suavis* comes from Java and Bali.

VERBENA
Verbena, Vervain

The verbena, a native of South and Central America, appreciates a location in full sunlight to semi-shade, at the very least. It will reward you for this by producing countless fragrant blossoms from the late spring until well into the autumn. Its flowers, which form thick, umbel-like flower heads, may be white, violet or blue, depending upon the variety. There are very beautiful hanging types as well as upright varieties; you can also cultivate the verbena as a high-stemmed plant. The verbena can tolerate relatively low temperatures, however, it is not frost-resistant.

Water the plant regularly and thoroughly in summer; in cold weather, just enough that the flowers do not wilt.

The verbena requires a dose of fertiliser every ten days beginning in midsummer.

Propagate via seeds.

Species and Types

Verbena canadensis, V. rigida, 'Novalis', 'Blaze', 'Amore', 'Gartenparty', 'Weisser Zwerg'.

Try re-cultivating your verbena every summer using cuttings. If you keep the young plants over the winter, you will have new, abundantly growing plants in the following season.

VIOLA CORNUTA
Viola, Horned violet, Tufted pansy, Johnny jump-up

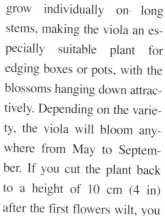

If you follow a few simple care guidelines, the viola can be a rewarding perennial ornament for your patio or balcony. Its little flowers may be red, yellow, purple or white. They grow individually on long stems, making the viola an especially suitable plant for edging boxes or pots, with the blossoms hanging down attractively. Depending on the variety, the viola will bloom anywhere from May to September. If you cut the plant back to a height of 10 cm (4 in) after the first flowers wilt, you can stimulate it to bloom a second time.

The delicate viola is appropriate as a potted flower, but also as a bedding plant. If you grow your violas—which are actually winter hardy—in a pot, they will need to be protected from frost. You will need to think carefully about the best location for your them.

This plant loves a bright location—no more than slightly shady—but it should not be placed in the bright midday sun. The number of flowers that the plant produces corresponds directly to the amount of light it receives.

The viola appreciates a regular watering schedule. If the substrate becomes too dry, the roots will die off. Begin fertilising one month after planting. Propagate via seeds or through division.

VRIESEA SPLENDENS
Flaming sword

This magnificent bromeliad is a native of Brazil, where it lives as an epiphyte. Its large, funnel-shaped rosettes consist of leaves that are up to 50 cm (20 in) long, with striking, brown, diagonal stripes; green-leaved varieties also exist.

Water collects in the centre of the rosette, in the so-called vase. Unfortunately, each rosette blooms only once. The flaming sword and its relatives look very attractive when placed on an epiphyte stalk.

This bromeliad requires a semi-shady location that receives some sun every day, as well as high humidity and warm temperatures throughout the year.

A flaming sword needs soil consistently moistened with soft, room temperature water. Water the plant into the funnel as well as on the root ball. Fertilise lightly with lime-free fertiliser every two weeks in the summer.

Propagate via offshoots: the young rosettes should remain attached to the parent plant for approximately six months.

Varieties and Other Species
'Major'. *Vriesa psittacina*: wide, oval-shaped, multicoloured inflorescence; delicate, light green leaf rosette.

YUCCA
Yucca

One of our most beloved indoor trees is the yucca, a native of the semi-desert regions of Central America. Although it is actually a member of the agave family, it is frequently identified as a palm because of its palm-like tufts of leaves. This decorative, exotic-looking plant is very robust and grows rapidly.

The yucca's needs a bright, sunny, airy and warm spot in summer—ideally outdoors. In winter, keep it in a bright, cool, frost-free room.

Water generously in summer if it is kept outdoors; moderately if in the house. In winter, water only moderately at low temperatures. Fertilise about every two weeks in summer; re-pot every two to three years in spring.

Propagate by rooting sections of the trunk or using side runners: conditions should be very humid and warm.

Species

Yucca aloifolia: stiff, dagger-shaped leaves with sharp points arranged in dense rosettes; interesting structured trunk with leaf patterns. *Y. elephantipes*, spineless yucca: its thick, tuber-like trunk remains close to the ground; the plant forms many side runners; sword-shaped leaves with non-pointed tips; coloured-leaf varieties also exist. Less common species are *Y. baccata, Y. brevifolia* and *Y. elata.*

ZANTEDESCHIA AETHIOPICA
Calla lily, Arum lily

This South African marsh plant, a member of the arum lily family, bears yellow spadices and smooth, wide leaves on its tall, upright stems. Each spadix is surrounded by an elegant white spathe.

Keep the calla lily in a bright, cool room during growth and flowering periods; it blooms in the early spring. It requires a rest period after blooming, during which the flowers will die off. You should permit the plant this rest even if it is kept outdoors (it also takes a rest period in its natural habitat). Keep the calla lily completely dry in a sunny location—preferably outdoors—from May through July.

Re-pot after the rest period, water generously, and fertilise once a week until the next flowers appear.

Propagate via division.

Species and Types

'Green Goddess': ivory and green spathe. *Zantedeschia elliottiana*: yellow flowers, wide, heart-shaped leaves. *Z. rehmannii*: white-purple at first, blooms violet-purple.

Wilting leaves and rotting tubers are a sign of a bacterial infection in the tubers. You can combat a mild attack using a copper solution. If the plant is heavily damaged, it will need to be destroyed.

PICTURE CREDITS

MEV, Augsburg (1)
Pflanzenbildarchiv MFW, Basel (30)
PhotoPress GmbH, Stockdorf (12)
Wolfgang Redeleit, Bienenbüttel (74)
Silvestris Fotoservice, Kastl (153)